5,00

A PUBLICATION FROM
THE JAMES FORD BELL COLLECTION IN THE
UNIVERSITY OF MINNESOTA LIBRARY

VAN METEREN'S

Virginia

1607–1612

by JOHN PARKER

UNIVERSITY OF MINNESOTA PRESS · MINNEAPOLIS

TO

James Ford Bell

MERCHANT · COLLECTOR
· PATRON OF LEARNING ·

PREFACE

THE story of Virginia's early years, the seedtime of our nation, is a chapter in Anglo-American history that has not wanted for distinguished historians. The three centuries that separate the writings of Captain John Smith from those of Thomas J. Wertenbaker produced innumerable histories, articles, monographs, and collections of sources to chronicle and document the beginnings of this republic.

It was not merely an Anglo-American story, however, for other nations looked on with interest or jealousy, and some were on the brink of involvement during the first half dozen years when the survival of the colony seemed indeed improbable. The Dutch historian Emanuel van Meteren was one who took note of those early years from London, and he recorded both his observations and his opinions in his great *History of the Netherlands*, which was very popular on the Continent and which was, therefore, a very early non-English source of information for Europeans about the English colony in America.

My purpose here is to present Van Meteren's views on the Virginia enterprise from its beginnings to his death on April 8, 1612, against the background of both the Anglo-Dutch friendship which prevailed during his lifetime and the rivalry which was constantly present and which would cause the dissolution of that friendship later in the seventeenth century.

A good bibliography of Van Meteren's *History* does not yet exist.

There are many difficulties facing the bibliographer who would undertake the task, for many of the editions are undated, Van Meteren was constantly adding material to his book, and some of the editions are exceedingly rare. In preparing this book I have used primarily the 1609 and 1614 Dutch and the 1612 German editions, of which there are copies in the Bell Collection at the University of Minnesota Library, but I have also had access to other printings through the courtesy of the Library of Congress, the British Museum, and the New York Historical Society. In the use of additional contemporary works I have appreciated the cooperation of the Folger, Huntington, John Carter Brown, Newberry, and Princeton University libraries. A leave of absence granted by the University of Minnesota gave me the opportunity to do much of my research in the British Museum and the Public Record Office.

In presenting a Dutch view of the Virginia story I have needed and appreciated the linguistic help of Mr. Hugh Olmsted and Mr. Simon M. Namenwirth. Mr. K. M. Hesselbach rendered special assistance in searching for particular documents in the Algemeen Rijks Archief in The Hague, and Mr. A. Gerrits supplied useful information on some of the early editions of Van Meteren's *History*. My major indebtedness in this work, however, is to the staff and resources of the University of Minnesota Library.

JOHN PARKER

April 8, 1961

TABLE OF CONTENTS

Van Meteren's Virginia

THE ANGLO-DUTCH ALLIANCE

THERE are few Dutch remains on the eastern shore of North America between thirty-four and forty-five degrees north latitude, Virginia's first boundaries, to give physical evidence of the interest and intentions of the young republic of the United Netherlands during its emergence as a colonial power. But its brief success in this part of the New World has left a very clear imprint on the American mind — we readily conjure up an image of peg-legged Peter Stuyvesant thumping about New Amsterdam in the last days that it wore a Dutch name, or a picture of the unloading from a Dutch ship of the first African slaves on our soil at Jamestown. The little *Halve Maen* under its English commander nosing up New York's river toward where Troy now stands, the *Mayflower* and its emigrant Pilgrims from Leiden, these too form a part of that memory of things Dutch in our past. And when John Adams, United States ambassador to the Dutch republic, sought an alliance with that country in 1781, he recalled to his hearers in the States-General the similarities in government and religion that bound the Dutch and American peoples, dwelt on their comparable attitudes toward personal freedom, and noted the similar circumstances under which the two republics were born.[1]

The "similitudes" Adams pointed out did produce a bond warm and lasting between the two peoples. But this was not a simple matter of direct influence. The similarities owed less to the brief hour of Dutch planting between Hudson and Stuyvesant than to the fact that the Eng-

[3

lish who replaced the Dutch with such apparent finality in 1664 had close religious and political ties of their own to their neighbor on the Continent, and were in fact deeply indebted to the Netherlanders for much that brought them success in both commerce and Colonial enterprises.[2]

In view of the common concerns of Englishmen and Dutchmen at the time both were beginning colonies abroad, which led them into a brief period of virtual partnership, it was natural that Emanuel van Meteren, a Dutch merchant living in London, should take a deep interest in the beginnings of English colonization in Virginia, and should record some of the earliest events in the history of that colony. It was in Virginia that the need for Anglo-Dutch collaboration seemed most necessary to some of the imperialists in both countries, and we shall see in later chapters how Van Meteren reflected in his notes the problems and uncertainties of the partnership, as well as the hopes. But first we must examine briefly the historic relationship between the two peoples by way of setting the scene for consideration of Van Meteren's Virginia.

The commercial tie across the "narrow sea" was an ancient one, for from medieval times English commerce found its best market for wool in the Low Countries, and the importance of this market to England grew, giving rise to a saying common in Antwerp that "If English men's fathers were hanged at Andwarpes gates, their children to come into that towne would creepe betwixt their legges."[3] If the English were aware of this dependence, they were also aware that the clothiers of the Netherlands must look to them for raw wool. The author of *The Libelle of Englyshe Polycye* reminded the merchants of Antwerp in 1436 that their vaunted prosperity was based upon English goods:

> The grete substaunce of youre cloothe at the fulle
> Ye wot ye make hit of our English wolle.[4]

This implied the power to throttle Flemish prosperity should the English wish to do so, and the idea of economic coercion seems to have had some appeal to the author as he wrote:

They may not lyven to mayntene there degrees
Wythoughten oure Englyshe commodytees,
Wolle and tynne, for the wolle of Englonde
Susteyneth the comons Flemmynges I understonde.
Thane, yf Englonde wolde hys wolle restrayne
From Flaundres, thys foloweth in certayne,
Flaundres of nede muste wyth us have pease
Or ellis he is distroyde wythowghten lees.[5]

Whatever the feelings of superiority by the Antwerpers and of hostility by the English (attitudes not unnatural in a commercial relationship which brings a rustic supplier into contact with a more sophisticated and wealthy manufacturer), this was an association that brought advantage to both parties and was of decided long-run benefit to England, for it enabled this insular nation to learn in commerce from one of Europe's most internationally minded people. In the crafts, in art, in science, and in business the Dutch were the teachers, the English the pupils. Frequently the teaching was done on the pupil's soil, for Flemish weavers began to arrive in England shortly after the Norman conquest.

Like the Norman rulers, the Flemish weavers in time became English, but a continuing stream of new migrants kept the English ever conscious of a foreign element among them, of people whose talents enriched the nation but aroused resentment in the less skilled English cloth worker who had to compete with the newcomers. Other aspects of the English economy felt the impact of Dutch enterprise also, for Dutch ships took much of England's wool to the Continent, and fishermen from the Low Countries supplied many an English town with fish from English coastal waters.

In the fourteenth century Edward III, recognizing that in both migration and trade the initiative lay with the Netherlanders, sought to improve his nation's position by actively encouraging Flemish craftsmen to settle in England, instead of merely permitting them to migrate as his predecessors had done. The result was a movement to England of weavers, dyers, and fullers larger in volume than ever before.[6] Then too English manufacturers of cloth shortly made technological changes in their industry, even going outside of the traditional guilds to improve their competitive position. By the end of the Middle Ages the master responded with attempts to exclude the student's cloth.[7] England's knowledge of commerce grew also, and English carriers entered more actively into the transporting of wool to the Netherlands for processing.

The competition that grew up in manufacturing and trade had in it elements of nationalism which would ultimately set these two nations against each other in a series of wars remarkable both for their intensity and their lack of ideological conflict. A foreshadowing of the coming contest can be seen in the continued resentment toward the Netherlander in England by certain of his hosts. "Shoulder of mutton and English beer make the Flemings tarry here" was a frequent English taunt pointing to the materialism of the Dutch.

Yet more than mutton and beer were gladly supplied by the English yeomen on the rise who saw to it that the immigrant weavers' "beds should be good and their bedfellows better"[8] as they sought out advantageous marriages for their daughters. Such marriage ties, fostered by the commercial interdependence of the two peoples, were one of the forces of friendship that were much more telling in the sixteenth century than the budding rivalries. Common cultural interests too were a factor of significance.

Both the Netherlanders and the English had come under strong French influence, making the culture of each meaningful to the other.[9] Continued Dutch settlement in various parts of England and the practice of sending young Englishmen to the Low Countries to learn manners as well as commerce nourished a long tradition of cultural interchange begun before the Normans came to England. Saxons from Britain had supplied the first bishops of Utrecht, the early religious center of the Netherlands.[10] Dutch students had traveled to Jarrow and York in the time of Bede and Alcuin, and later when the Danes made England less hospitable to scholars, the Netherlands had received English scholars in its centers of learning.[11] During the six centuries and more of Dutch primacy the Netherlands gave to English thought and letters *The Imitation of Christ, Everyman, Reynard the Fox,* and *Mary of Nemmegen.* It sent Caxton back to England a printer, and Wynkyn de Worde followed him shortly. It gave Erasmus to England, where he learned as well as taught, and where his influence was strong and abiding in intellectual circles. Dutch appreciation of English interests is shown by the willingness of Dutch booksellers to invest in books for the English market.[12] The first English account of the New World came from the press of Jan van Doesborch between 1511 and 1520 bearing the title *Of the Newe Landes . . .* and it is understandable that Sir Thomas More should have sent his *Utopia* to Louvain for its first printing, and, indeed, that the dialogue should have been set in Antwerp.

In view of this easy intellectual relationship between the two peoples, the publication of the first English Bible by a Dutchman in Antwerp, Jacob van Meteren, is not surprising. It was in the realm of religion, in fact, that the English and Netherlandish peoples were drawn most closely together. The ingredients of the Reformation were present in both countries as far back as the fourteenth century, and if England's skies were not lighted in the 1520's with fires from the stake, as were those over the Netherlands, the question of what a man might believe was nevertheless an ever-present issue in Henry VIII's domain. Tyndale's translation of the New Testament had to be smuggled into his homeland, and official hostility to Protestants drove many reformers to the Continent. Among those who fled was Miles Coverdale, who translated the Bible which Jacob van Meteren published in 1535.[13] With the coming of the English Reformation, the ties of commerce and literature which had brought the two countries to close understanding were supplemented by the strong bond of common revolt against old forms and authorities, a revolt at once intellectual and emotional, religious and national.

As anti-Lutheran edicts, backed by burnings and hangings at the hands of Spanish administrators, made themselves felt in the Netherlands, England became a haven of refuge and many Dutch merchants fled across the North Sea. About 15,000 of them were in England in

1527.[14] Some managed to bring their money with them, all brought their skills and their reformed religion. These migrants settled primarily in London, a city generally hospitable to them, although not officially sharing their faith. Their right to separate existence as a religious body was recognized in 1550 when they were granted the use of the Church of the Austin Friars by the king. Here they organized under the leadership of Johannes a Lasco, a Polish nobleman and onetime friend of Erasmus. As the migration continued, other Dutch communities developed at Norwich, Maidstone, Sandwich, Colchester, Stamford, Thetford, and Dover.[15]

Among the migrants coming to London around the middle of the century was Emanuel van Meteren, son of the publisher. He had been born in Antwerp on July 9, 1535, at a time when a Protestant father might well have been looking to England not only for business but for asylum for his family. It was not until 1550, however, that Jacob van Meteren, then himself temporarily in London, proposed to his son that he come to England to study theology under Emanuel Tremillius, a friend of Calvin's and professor of Hebrew at Cambridge. But the boy indicated a preference for business, and when he arrived in London it was as an apprentice to Sebastaen Danckerts, an Antwerp merchant resident in London. By this time his schooling had included study in Antwerp, Tournay, and Duffel, and though he had but small talent for Latin, his interest in other subjects must have been lively, for throughout his life Emanuel van Meteren was a tireless collector of coins, signatures, pamphlets, and sheer information. An acute mind must also have found abundant stimulation in a household where the father's publishing interests kept him abreast of the latest religious thinking, and the mother, Ottilia Ortels van Meteren, was a member of the family that gave to her son's generation the great map publisher Abraham Ortelius.[16]

After Jacob and Ottilia van Meteren were drowned in 1552 as they too were moving to London, young Emanuel was drawn close to his famous cousin Abraham, and their correspondence reveals their joint interest in medals and books and in the news that flowed into London and

Antwerp from other places. Though apprenticed to a merchant, Emanuel's chief love was history, and a companion apprentice remembered years later how they had resented business chores that kept them from learned pursuits, "the hankering for which we relieved by mutual complaints and discussions of our stealthy studies." [17]

Although he may have come to regret his earlier decision to forsake Cambridge theology for London counting, Emanuel van Meteren was a successful businessman, and his talents were quickly recognized by others, for he was appointed a factor to several merchants about 1560. This was the first step toward his ultimate appointment as consul to Antwerp merchants in London in 1583, a position he held until his death in 1612. In this latter capacity he formed a wide acquaintance among both Englishmen and Netherlanders, giving and receiving information, and doing favors of all sorts, like many a consul before and since. We find Jacob Cool writing to Ortelius from London, "My mother says that she forgot to write to my aunt that we had received the buckwheat sent by her through Emanuel van Meteren," [18] and other letters tell of similar duties performed by the consul.

As a man of affairs and learning, Van Meteren could not but be aware of the forces coming to the surface in English life. The growth of Puritanism, the increasing hostility to Spain, and the beginnings of the imperialistic urge were major components of the English intellectual and political climate. They struck a sympathetic chord in Van Meteren too, for these same forces were at the base of Dutch patriotism.

The strength of Puritanism was augmented in England in the 1560's as Dutch immigrants came by the thousands, bringing with them memories of greater numbers who met death for heresy in their own country. These memories did not lessen the heresy of the immigrants; they did not come meekly, seeking shelter only, but rather brandished an aggressive faith. Their example was not wasted on many Englishmen who were discontented with the religious forms decreed by the Crown. The intellectual capital of the dissidents was Cambridge. There the English and Dutch shared their Calvinism, as members of the Dutch community in

London subscribed to funds to send as many of their youth to Cambridge as possible. Emanuel van Meteren is listed as a subscriber to this fund in 1575, 1581, and 1591.[19] It was at Cambridge that Thomas Cartwright, in 1569, gave lectures to the effect that Scripture alone should determine what was obligatory in the Church, and when he was expelled from the university for such opinions he moved to Antwerp where he preached to a congregation of English merchants.[20]

Although the faith of these extremists was not sanctioned by the Crown, there were officials in high places with kindly feelings toward the Dutch Protestants who proposed to continue the Reformation in England. If Queen Mary sent some of them into exile along with many of her own subjects, her successor said, "We approve your ceremonies inasmuch as they accord best with the countries whence you came." [21] This tolerant attitude was apparent in the actions of Edmund Grindal, then bishop of London and the nominal superior of the Dutch Protestants, who pleaded for unity among them after factionalism broke out, and even tried to extend English protection to their brethren abroad when in 1561 he urged upon Frankfurt toleration of Dutch refugees there who were being "set upon by some zealous Lutherans." [22]

Such sympathic views permitted Dutch Calvinism to survive in England. Meanwhile it was surviving in the Netherlands too, for Dutch revulsion against Spanish administration and Spanish persecution forged a rebellion in 1565 that cleared the northern provinces of Spaniards and by 1589 established the authority of the States-General, a loose governing body, many of whose members were Calvinists, over this area. Now when the spirit of dissent in England spawned sects which were not tolerated there, they looked to the Netherlands for refuge. Robert Brown, for example, whose studies at Cambridge and life among the Dutch refugees in Norwich led him to found a sect of Separatists, settled his following in Amsterdam in 1593. From this group, some of whom moved to Leiden in 1609, came the founders of the Baptist church in England as a few of them moved back to their native land with a new Dutch religion.

10]   The Netherlands was not merely a haven for oppressed Englishmen,

it was an example and an inspiration to Englishmen concerned with the survival of the Protestant religion. Indeed it was the Dutch war of liberation that stood as the watershed between Spanish power and decline. And one did not even have to be a Puritan to be on the side of the Netherlanders, for they were resisting the national enemy of England, the enemy of the queen and her church as well as the foe of the more extreme Protestants. The English followed the Dutch war of liberation in the 1560's, 70's, and 80's with intense interest as it became increasingly clear that the struggle across the North Sea was England's war also. In fact the Low Countries became an outlet for belligerent English Protestantism, and there its champions tested their sinews alongside troops pledged to endure every hardship to achieve victory. To this conflict such men of literary talent as Gascoigne, Churchyard, Marlowe, Sidney, and Ben Jonson were drawn, and there was a deep public interest in pamphlets describing the conflict and in inflammatory tracts which left no doubt of the danger England was in.

The anti-Spanish mood fed upon English conflict with the Spaniards elsewhere also. Englishmen read of Sir John Hawkins's "miseries and troublesome affayres" during his defeat at San Juan de Ullua;[23] they saw their queen, with typical aggressiveness where money was concerned, lay hold of Spanish treasure ships driven into English ports; they plotted briefly with French Protestants to set up a colony in Florida where Spanish ships could be raided regularly as they returned from Spanish America.

Hatred for Spain led many a pamphleteer and soldier farther toward alliance with the Netherlands than did the actions of the shrewd virgin who spoke for England. She was not entirely a spectator, but she was not a partner until it became quite necessary. She ordered Dutch refugees to spread out across the country so that there would be no concentrated settlements to give obvious evidence of her sympathy with them. She refused the sovereignty of Holland and Zeeland when it was offered by representatives of those provinces. A loan to the Netherlands was secured by the English garrisoning of certain Dutch cities, and military support was tied to the right of the commander of such troops to sit and vote in the Netherlands Council of State.[24] By 1585, however, it was clear that the Dutch could not survive without assistance more generously given. Antwerp had fallen, William of Orange had been assassinated, and Dutch negotiations with France were unproductive and unpopular. But in the shadow of the Spanish noose the Dutch and English friends quibbled over rights of sovereignty before an agreement providing for English assistance could be effected. And when eventually English troops under the Earl of Leicester fought on Dutch soil, there were bickerings and suspicions.

Nevertheless, the common enemy was not forgotten, and in the eyes of Emanuel van Meteren, making observations on the Dutch war of liberation from his vantage point in London, the great Spanish Armada of 1588, so well remembered in English naval annals, was equally directed against the Netherlands, and "was intended for their ruine and destruction." [25] It was also, in his view, an assault on the Anglo-Dutch alliance and the Protestant religion the partners upheld. "It was the expedition which the Spanish king, having a long time determined the same in his minde, and having consulted thereabout with the Pope, set foorthe and undertooke against England and the low Countreys. To the ende that he might subdue the realme of England, and reduce it unto his catholique Religion . . ." [26] Throughout his account of the preparations and battle Van Meteren shifted the narrative from England to the Netherlands and back. Although the action concerned English ships primarily, he recorded that "the shippes of Holland and Zeland stood continually in their [Spanish] sight, threatening shot and powder, and many inconveniences unto them." [27]

In this great test of strength England and the Netherlands stood closer together than they ever had before. Together they prayed for victory for the Protestant cause, and it is possible to believe that an Anglo-Dutch state of mind existed, for each nation alone was inadequate to the task of preserving its independence and each knew it. Van Meteren's account of the Armada suggests such a state of mind, and Richard Hakluyt, one of England's foremost nationalists, must have seen the battle in the same light, for when he published an account of it ten years later, the first in the English language, it was a translation of Van Meteren's description of the great victory that he used. When it was over and the queen had given her people a day of thanksgiving, and the Zeelanders had struck a medal in honor of the victory, poetry eulogized the victorious sovereign, some of it, with such thoughts as these, surely approved by thankful Dutchmen:

> And now, O Queen, above all others blest,
> For whom both windes and waves are prest to fight,
> So rule your owne, so succour friends opprest,
> (As farre from pride, as ready to do right)
> That England you, and you England long enjoy
> No less your friends delight, then foes annoy.[28]

Yet in the following decade, English assistance was grudgingly given to the Dutch, and was frequently received with complaints. While many men of Van Meteren's generation may have found it impossible to imagine a world in which everything they cherished would not be threatened by Spain, making the alliance a necessity for all but eternity, there were those who felt as Leicester was supposed to have expressed it: ". . . these legges of mine shall never goe againe into Holland, lett the States gett other to serve their mercenary turne if they will to make themselves rich, for me they shall not have." [29]

While the English complained about the mercenary nature of the Dutch, and Van Meteren observed of the English that they "are not so laborious and industrious as the Netherlanders or the French," [30] both nations by the last years of the sixteenth century were launched on courses of empire that were primarily mercenary in purpose.

From about midcentury a few "obscure members of the commonwealth," to use Richard Eden's term, had pleaded with little success for an active policy of English overseas expansion, and they had supplied English readers with navigation books and accounts of distant regions translated from other languages.[31] Among the enthusiasts for empire were many of the same literary figures who had served against Spain in the Low Countries.

The Dutch were not free to pursue such dreams in the 1570's and 1580's, but they were awake to the rustlings of imperialism in Europe. Antwerp, the major printing center of the Low Countries, saw the publication of many descriptions of the Spanish Empire; Abraham Ortelius published his great atlas there in 1570; the important collection of voyages first published by Simon Grynaeus in 1532 achieved its most complete edition in the Dutch printing of 1563;[32] and while France, England, Portugal, and Spain were claiming the New World, it was Corneille Wytfliet who in Louvain published the first atlas of the New World in 1597.[33]

By the 1590's, when the northern provinces had won their independence from Spain, the Dutch were ready to give free reign to their aggressive mercantile tendencies. They learned of the East Indies in the masterly *Itinerario* of Jan Huygen van Linschoten, published in 1596,[34] and before the end of the century they were sending fleets of ships to tap the spice trade long regarded as the preserve of the Portuguese and Spanish. Voyages by the Strait of Magellan and attempts to find a northeast passage were also made before 1600. Dutch imperialism was born full-grown.

Accounts of these voyages were quickly translated into English, largely through the urging of Richard Hakluyt, and the English were aroused to a fever pitch to emulate their mercenary neighbors. They had made attempts in 1591 and 1596 to establish trade with the East Indies, but both voyages had ended in disaster.[35] Now disaster of a more permanent kind threatened, for the English Levant commerce could not prosper in competition with the Dutch who traded directly with the East Indies, gathering at their source the commodities from the East needed in western Europe. It became imperative that an English company be established to trade with the East Indies also. While the queen hesitated to license a company that would surely offend Spain even as she was trying to restore peace, the pressure mounted for merchants to pay up their

14]

subscriptions, dockmen to ready the ships, and sailors to get under way.[36] A new rivalry was being born, a new century beginning, and yet it owed something to the earlier spirit, for both English and Dutch sought first the destruction of the Spanish and Portuguese trade in the East Indies. When the fleet of the newly formed East India Company finally departed from Woolwich on February 13, 1601, one of its leaders was John Davis, England's foremost pilot, who had made the voyage five years earlier in a Dutch ship.

The advocates of empire in England had always told themselves that their natural province for exploration was to the northwest, and one of the first actions of the East India Company was to send George Weymouth in search of a northwest passage in 1602. In the century that separated Weymouth's failure from that of Cabot, English captains had tried several times to find a northwest passage, and they had become acquainted with the North American coasts in their search. Exploration was never completely separated from the idea of colonizing, but the royal attitude was one of hesitancy toward the establishment of settlements which would invite the hostility of Spain. Raleigh's little colony at Roanoke perished while England was winning its great victory over the Armada, and after the victory there was neither royal policy nor popular clamor for colonies in North America. When the great queen died in 1603 she had not even the beginnings of an empire in America, only a group of free-lance merchants and fishermen, learning the geography and economy of North America's coast.

There were forces at work, however, to quicken English interest in colonizing this area just as there had been in the East Indies. By 1603 Champlain was in America to bring order to French trade in the St. Lawrence River. By this time the Dutch too were beginning to show an interest in Newfoundland, although more as traders than as fishermen. And in these early years of the new century the first prophet of the Dutch West India Company was heard preaching the advantages of a strong commercial organization in the New World. Willem Usselinx, merchant of Antwerp and implacable foe of Spain, was familiar with the trade of the West Indies from several years' experience in the Azores. He had begun about 1600 to write down some of his ideas for establishing Dutch commerce in the New World in preparation for an intensive pamphleteering campaign that was to follow.[37]

Usselinx was no idle dreamer. In a country where only old men could remember peace with Spain the transfer of some of the Dutch war of liberation to the New World was certain to find advocates — and to Antwerpers the war of liberation could not end until their city was as free as the northern provinces. The success of the East India merchants made a similar plan for American trade seem plausible, especially since the homeland of Mercator, Ortelius, and Plancius was a storehouse of the best available information on the geography of America. The ingredients of a successful American enterprise were present in the Netherlands, and as England buried the queen who had brought her nation to the brink of empire, the little band of imperialists there might well have pondered whether she had waited too long.

The East and West Indies, arousing visions of empire in England and the Netherlands, presented opportunities for joint action against the Iberian hegemony. They also were arenas where Anglo-Dutch mercantile bickerings of the past could be continued on a grand scale. As both nations advanced to the frontiers of imperialism, Emanuel van Meteren, an old man now, and still living in London, recorded the closing events of the century of Anglo-Dutch cooperation, and the beginning of their century of conflict.

His original intention had been to gather material to be given to a historian who would write a history of the Netherlands, particularly of the war of liberation.[38] But in the late 1580's when Frans Hogenberg, a publisher in Cologne, asked Ortelius where material might be found to go along with engravings he had for an illustrated history of the Dutch war, the famous map publisher thought of his cousin in London. Van Meteren sent his manuscript to Hogenberg, and upon the death of that publisher, his stepson issued the plates and Van Meteren's text, translated into German. Although there was no indication of date, or of place, publisher, or privilege, this edition actually appeared in 1593.[39] Thus began the history of a book that was to know innumerable editions. In 1596 a Second Part was published, and later that year the two parts appeared in a one-volume edition. It was reprinted in 1597 and 1598, and in the latter year a Latin edition was published.[40]

The obvious popularity of the book made it natural for Van Meteren to want a Dutch edition, and this thought was also on the mind of Cornelisz Vennecool, a publisher in Delft, who obtained a privilege for the publication of a Dutch edition in 1597. Van Meteren and Vennecool had at least as many difficulties as are common in author-publisher relationships. The author was unhappy that Vennecool received the privilege in the first place, and secured an agreement from the States-General that they would appoint a supervisor to watch over the publication. Vennecool wanted merely to translate the text back into Dutch out of German, but Van Meteren insisted on an entirely new edition. The author continued to send in material for inclusion, and the publisher was understandably anxious to get on with the printing. Finally it was finished and presented to the States-General in 1599. The delegates refused to accept it, for despite their nominal supervision of the book's publication it offended both moderates and Calvinists in that body, as well as others who criticized its accuracy. The States-General forbade its distribution in the Netherlands, and as a final frustration to the author, Vennecool neglected to send him a copy of the book.[41]

Despite all these difficulties with his book, Van Meteren continued to gather material for new editions which appeared in Dutch, Latin, and German to the end of his life, and it was the later issues that chronicled the beginnings of English colonization in Virginia.

Even in its earliest editions, Van Meteren's *History* was not confined entirely to the history of the Netherlands. Because he saw the English conflict with Spain as a part of the Dutch war of liberation, he found it easy to include Drake's West India voyage of 1585, the capture of Spanish galleons by the English in 1592, and the West Indian raid of 1595 by Hawkins and Drake. He did not, however, describe Raleigh's Virginia or Guiana undertakings, except to note that Drake stopped at Virginia on his way home from the West Indies and rescued some Englishmen who had been abandoned by their friends.[42] This appears to be a criticism of the faintheartedness of the English in failing to support their first Virginia Colony.

In these years of recording Dutch and English overseas activities, Van Meteren was also an intermediary who could be of assistance to both countries. We know of an instance in 1594 when certain merchants of Zeeland sought his aid in locating someone who could give them the most expert information on the northeast passage; Van Meteren recommended his old friend Richard Hakluyt, who supplied the information, and it was put to use when Willem Barents attempted to find a northeast passage in voyages of 1595 and 1596.[43]

As historian and intermediary, interesting himself in the new opportunities for trade and empire that both countries were exploring, Van Meteren exemplifies the cooperative spirit that prevailed in large measure between the Dutch and English during his lifetime.

BEGINNINGS IN VIRGINIA

EMANUEL VAN METEREN and his Dutch colleagues in London should have found no cause to worry over the future of their good relations with the English sovereign at the accession of Scotland's James VI to England's throne as James I, for on May 23, 1603, he promised the aliens in England his protection, noting the contributions they had made to English life.[1] He assured the foreign churches in England of his favorable disposition toward them. He even gave momentary hope to the English Puritans that they too might find favor with him, and thus be permitted to act on their Calvinistic beliefs as freely as the Dutch. But these were false signs, for James had two ambitions which acted as powerful cross currents to the flow of sentiment that had produced Anglo-Dutch unity.

It was a fundamental tenet of James's political philosophy that good order in the state could be achieved only if the ultimate political authority was vested in a king ruling by divine right. The alternative was absolute disorder. And he believed that good national order required royal supervision of religious matters as well as political, which was to be accomplished through the king's appointment of bishops. To James the position of the Puritans in matters of church government appeared to foreshadow a presbytery, which "agreeth with a monarchy as God and the Devil."[2] The king listened to clerical views on the relationship of church to state at the Hampton Court conference, called in 1604 to permit Puritan preachers to air their grievances; he saw nothing in these views but danger to the order he cherished and thundered his classic "No bishop, no king." He followed with a logical warning, "I will make them [Puritans] conform or I will harry them out of this land or else do worse." [3] In giving this notice, James was announcing a lack of sympathy for a major ingredient of the Anglo-Dutch alliance.

The other major bond of Anglo-Dutch unity, opposition to Spain, was to be severed with less argument, but no less purpose. James viewed himself as the potential messiah of peace, the leader of the Protestant countries *and* the friend of those bearing allegiance to Rome. From this lofty position he extended the hand of fellowship to Spain, the enemy of every English and Dutch patriot, the tyrant state that had hoped to reduce both England and the Netherlands to subservience. The Dutch had agreed to make no important moves in foreign policy without England's consent, but James felt free to go to the peace table in August 1604 without showing the least regard even for the feelings of his country's ally. He promised Spain that England would lend no more aid to the Dutch rebels, and then with fine impartiality made it possible for both countries to recruit troops to their cause in England. Elizabeth had been aware that there was no hope of ending the war with Spain through more war. But the manner in which James made peace served abrupt notice upon the Netherlands that as far as the Crown of England was concerned, its former ally held no favored position in its struggle with Spain, but was in fact deep in England's debt even to the extent that the towns of Rammekens, Flushing, and Brill were to continue in English hands.

Now the Dutch fought on alone, but not entirely alone, for there were still those in England whose sympathies remained firm despite the change in policy by the new monarch. Further, the king of Spain did not find any enthusiasm for his cause among the English as the Gunpowder Plot renewed suspicion of Roman Catholicism, of which Spain was still regarded as champion. While bickering continued between English soldiers and their Dutch hosts,[4] hospitality prevailed at Portsmouth and the Isle of Wight in 1606, when a Dutch fleet just back from the coast of Spain was allowed to "trim and make clean." [5] The Dutch ambassador

Noel de Caron attempted to capitalize on this continuing friendship by trying to wheedle more assistance from James.[6]

In short, the old alliance was not yet dead, nor had the reason for it vanished.[7] Spain's power had been diminished by war, not by the peace treaty, and while Englishmen may have loved peace, peace did not induce them to love their enemy. James agreed to keep English ships out of the area of the New World under Spanish control, but he could not do so. As the number of Spanish ships in American waters gradually lessened, and preying upon them became a marginal enterprise, a clandestine trade, forbidden by both governments, was established in the Caribbean Sea by English ships frequently using Dutch registry and Dutch ports. James misjudged badly in measuring his treaty-enforcing power against the realities of commerce.

England was now stronger than Spain at sea, and not to take advantage of that strength seemed to many seagoing Englishmen a great error. Ferdinando Gorges, for one, did not see "whye his Highnesse may not make it free by his proclamation, for all his subjects to make warre in the Indes where he hath concluded noe peace, nor whether [sic] his subjects cannot goe but to their losse & ruen." [8] Frequent Spanish misdeeds were cited and there were suggestions that the Spanish were involved in "some plot on Ireland." [9]

Meanwhile the Spanish-controlled Portuguese East Indian empire was being penetrated by English and Dutch merchants, as both countries sent fleets there regularly in the first years of James's reign. In their East Indian factories the English and Dutch tolerated each other as necessity demanded. The Dutch were superior, and therefore the least tolerant. Both nations were anxious to remove Portuguese merchants from the competition, yet each was jealous of its own trade and its own reputation among the native peoples. There were instances of real cordiality, and there were signs of the inevitable conflict, as when the English merchants at Bantam very early had scarves made of red and white taffeta so that the natives might distinguish them from the Dutch who were stationed there.[10] The rivalry between the newcomers to the East Indies was, however, overshadowed by the larger struggle between the Dutch and the Portuguese, and news of Dutch victories in the area found a happy reception in England.[11] While the English took Portuguese ships where they could, the offensive at sea was largely in Dutch hands.

The success of the Dutch in the East Indies lent momentum to the move for a Dutch West India Company. Willem Usselinx had his plans well formulated, and as both an anti-Spanish maneuver and a plausible mercantile enterprise, establishment of the company found support among merchants, shipowners, and others who were interested in overseas trade and the spreading of Protestantism abroad. A charter was drafted, providing for the administration and financing of the company, and it was issued in 1607.[12] There was, however, a counterforce at work in the Netherlands, for advocates of peace appeared in the cities of the northern provinces.

The war in the Low Countries had heavily taxed Spain's resources and by 1606 her representatives were seeking a truce. A peace party in the Netherlands responded under the leadership of John van Oldenbarneveldt, pensionary of Rotterdam. He and his followers were content with the success of the revolution which had liberated seven provinces in the northern Netherlands, leaving them in loose confederation. They felt that further war would in all probability solidify the provinces into a state less easily dominated by the municipal oligarchies that controlled the States-General. Furthermore, the northern cities had gained in trade at the expense of Antwerp, which was blockaded, and its liberation might have adverse effects on their prosperity, for many an Antwerper who had gone into exile hoped to return with his capital and his mercantile abilities to restore the entrepôt on the Scheldt to its accustomed commercial supremacy. There were others who wanted peace simply out of weariness with the war, and the realization that any final settlement with Spain would have to be made at a peace table rather than on the battlefield. While there was hope of liberating a few more towns of the southern Netherlands, there was little prospect of dealing Spain a decisive defeat, especially after England had withdrawn from the war.

Mindful of its own power, the Netherlands proceeded into negotiations for a truce in 1607 without particular regard to England's wishes. As a result James grumbled at Dutch impulsiveness and failure to keep him advised as the treaty of 1585 provided.[13] His passion for peace was now put to the test, as Spanish envoys whispered to him of the impending danger from the control of the seas by the Dutch, and the Dutch themselves let it be known that they were not the satellites of England that James had assumed.[14] Would not England gain most if these two rivals fought each other to exhaustion? But since they had decided not to, James had to make the best he could of the situation and interest himself in the nature of the peace, if peace was indeed possible.

His representatives to the peace negotiations were Sir Ralph Winwood and Sir Richard Spencer. Strength in appearance but vagueness in policy was the core of their instructions as they were ordered to "demand an audience in the assemblie of the States Generall," and there to "speake in great termes" about England's interest in the settlement of the future of the Netherlands.[15] The Dutch were to be reminded of their own statement that they could not maintain the war alone; they were to be told that if war came out of the conference instead of peace, the Dutch alone, in England's view, could benefit. James urged resistance to any idea of a defensive league with the Dutch, and any talk of further assistance from England to the Dutch was ruled out on the basis of a depleted treasury, caused in part by this war which had been waged "merely for their sakes." [16]

Should the French show interest in becoming the principal ally of the Dutch, however, Spencer and Winwood were to leave the impression in French minds that England would stand by the Dutch in maintaining their freedom whether it be by peaceful means or by war.

The real issues of the negotiations were two: could the Dutch achieve the absolute independence they demanded for their liberated provinces, and could they continue to trade to the East and West Indies, areas which Spain claimed as her preserve? James gave no specific instructions on these points. He seems, rather, to have felt that peace alone would take care of both problems. He believed apparently that the Dutch states would not continue to be united after the cohesive force of war was replaced by pressures of self-interest, "the better sort of men being like to be wonne by corruption or ambition to change their fortunes," [17] and that the East Indian trade, deprived of its military motive, would not survive. James saw the Dutch war as the means by which the Netherlanders maintained their prosperity; peace, he felt, would bring ruin to their economy.

While misjudging the commercial strength of the Dutch, James probably had a more accurate impression of the military and naval strength of Spain. The helplessness of Spain's situation was indicated in the manner in which she looked to England in hope that somehow pressure could be brought upon the Dutch to moderate their demands on the two central issues,[18] and Ambassador Cornwallis confirmed it as he wrote from Madrid, "Our [the ambassador used "our" to refer to things Spanish] sea forces were never soe lame, and for lande services we were never worse furnisshed." [19]

James might well have wanted to throw his influence on the side of Spain against the Dutch, for a king believing in sovereignty by divine right cannot have been much in sympathy with a people who had just fought for half a century to rid themselves of a monarch. He was surely aware also that England's trade in the East Indies, which held promise of royal revenues, would have to compete with Dutch enterprise there. Yet any thoughts of friendship with Spain had to be considered in the light of English interest in the New World. While diplomats played their cautious game of war and peace, a little band of James's subjects, with his permission, set out for Virginia to fulfill Raleigh's prophecy "to see it an English nation." [20]

James had inherited no American territory with his crown, but found on his accession a vigorous Atlantic commerce which had grown up without any particular encouragement from the English government. Fishing voyages to Newfoundland and the New England region had grown steadily through the last part of the sixteenth century until by the end of Elizabeth's reign two hundred English vessels made the voyage to Newfoundland annually, and others called at Monhegan and Pemaquid on the Maine coast. The successful prosecution of fishing and fur trading [21] required permanent settlements, and following the Gosnold-Gilbert voyage of 1602, others of a reconnoitering nature followed under Martin Pring and Bartholomew Gosnold in 1603, and under George Weymouth in 1605. The area under study was "Virginia," the vast length of coastal land from Spanish Florida to Nova Scotia. Some of the place names these Englishmen, and their Dutch counterparts, gave to points along the coast are shown, in original spellings, on the map on page 28, which is intended to illustrate the appearance of the region as it attracted both Dutch and English explorers between 1606 and 1612. When a group of English merchants and promoters finally decided to plant a settlement there, and an organization was established to govern the enterprise, it was called the Council of Virginia.

The establishment of an English colony in Virginia could in no way be interpreted as a friendly act toward Spain, for the history of English activity in America to that time had been largely a record of despoiling Spanish possessions and raiding Spanish shipping. The Spanish government was well informed and deeply concerned about the new venture from the beginning. In a letter to his sovereign dated March 16, 1606, about three weeks before the Virginia charter was issued, Ambassador Pedro de Zuñiga wrote from London that the English were planning "to send 500 or 600 men, private individuals of this kingdom, to people Virginia in the Indies, close to Florida." [22] He went on to state that "the chief leader in this business is the Justiciario [Chief Justice, Sir John Popham] who is a very great Puritan." [23]

Dutch sympathizers were perhaps equally interested in the colony. It is easy to imagine the view that Emanuel van Meteren must have taken of this enterprise, a view which appeared to match that of his fellow Antwerper, Willem Usselinx: though peace at home might come to the Netherlands, here was an excellent opportunity to carry on the war with increased effectiveness from a base close to the heart of Spain's great source of wealth. It is not surprising, therefore, that Van Meteren, in gathering material for his book, should seek out some promoter of the colony, probably his friend Richard Hakluyt, and should receive from him a copy of the charter of the company, for it did not exist in published form in 1608 when the new edition of the *History of the Netherlands* [24] was being readied for publication. Van Meteren's abstract of the original charter, incorporated into his chronicle for the year 1607, was the first appearance in print of the first document relating to the Virginia colony. He added also some news of the first voyages to Virginia. A translation follows:

"In England this year two companies were established, to sail to and settle new lands, mostly through the urging of Richard Hakluyt, who had diligently described all the distant travels of the English, together with Sir John Popham, Chief Justice and Councilor of England. These men interested others in this project and received for this purpose patents from the king dated 10 April 1606.

"The first company was that of Thomas Gates, George Somers, knights, Richard Hakluyt, clerk, and Edward Maria Wingfield, together with other merchants of London. The second company was that of Thomas Hamond, Raleigh Gilbert, William Packer [Parker], and George Popham, with some others from the cities of Bristol, Exeter, and Plymouth. These men have full power and license from the king to go and live and settle the English colony in Virginia which is situated in America, was first discovered by the English, and is considered to belong to them, since it is not yet claimed by anyone else from Europe. It is, namely, the land stretching along the seacoast between thirty-four and forty-five degrees latitude north of the equinoctial line, and on the continent between thirty-four and forty-five degrees, and in the adjacent islands lying within one hundred miles.

"These two companies wished to divide it as follows: The one company, first named, that of Thomas Gates, etc., with those of London, would set themselves up in some good places along the coast between the thirty-fourth and forty-first degrees of the above mentioned latitude.

The second company, that of Thomas Hamond, etc., with those of Bristol, Exeter, and Plymouth, would establish themselves on the same coast of America somewhere between the thirty-eighth and forty-fifth degrees of the above mentioned latitude of the equinoctial line.

"This plan was highly commended by the king of Great Britain as a project that might in time greatly serve the honor and glory of God, the spreading of Christian religion, and the bringing of infidels to knowledge and civil behavior. He has granted and licensed their request by patent as follows: The first company may now begin establishing itself first between thirty-four and forty-one degrees, and take over all land, forests, harbors, rivers, fisheries, mines, etc., from where they first establish themselves to fifty miles along the coast to the west and southwest as the coasts lie, with all the islands lying opposite within one hundred miles, and similarly, from their first settlement fifty miles to the east and northeast. And so up to a hundred English miles inland they shall be permitted to remain living there, constructing and building and making fortifications for their protection at the discretion and direction of the council of the colony, and no one shall be permitted to live or establish himself thereabouts without express consent of the council of the same colony.

"A similar patent was also granted and licensed to the second company, that of Thomas Hamond, Raleigh Gilbert, William Packer [Parker], George Popham, with others from Bristol, Exeter, and Plymouth. They are to begin to settle, at their own initiative, between the thirty-eighth and forty-fifth degrees of the above mentioned latitudes, along the same coast of America to the west and southwest, or to the south as the coast lies, and similarly, all the islands situated within one hundred miles of the coast, and furthermore from their settlement fifty miles along the coast to the east and northeast or north as the coast shall lie, and so up to a hundred miles inland. All of this is on the condition that they shall settle and establish themselves here last, and that they shall not settle within one hundred English miles of the other colony which is first planted there. These colonies and planters, each from among them-

NEW FRANCE

NORUMBEGA

VIRGINIA

Moortreede Bay

Sagadahoc R.
Schoonhaven

Island of St. George
Gebroocken Hoek

Wyngaert Caep
Lichtmis Vaerdt
Kraenhaven
Whitson Bay
Cape Cod
Vlacke Hoeck

Manahata
Martha's
Vinyard

Colman's Point
Sasquasahanock R.

Chesiopook
Bay
Delaware Bay

Jamestown
De Droghe Caep
King's River
C. Henry
Hatorask
Roanoac
Croatoan

C. of Fear

Bermuda

ENGLISH AND DUTCH BEGINNINGS IN NORTH AMERICA,
1606–1612, FROM CONTEMPORARY MAPS AND NARRATIVES

selves, shall select a council of thirteen men, and have a seal bearing the king's coat of arms, and likewise with distinction between the first and second colony. These thirteen men shall have complete authority, following the ordinances, laws, and instructions that the king shall give under his hand and great seal. In England still another council of thirteen men shall reside called the King of Great Britain's Council of Virginia, with seal, etc.

"They all are to give the king a fifth of all gold and silver mined, and a fifteenth of other minerals. They may mint money there, and put to use what metals they wish. Also, they may bring people from England with all their goods and wares free of all duties for a period of seven years, with the restriction that no one may do so except members of the company, under forfeiture of ship and goods. Also, no one may settle there without license of the above mentioned colonies, and they have power to oppose all such with force and might. If any of the king's subjects want to trade there, the council may allow it upon payment of a duty of two and a half per cent, foreigners five per cent, and that profit is for the benefit of the company for twenty-one years of time, after which the duty will belong to the king. Children born there shall always be free English, and it is sharply forbidden to harm any friend at sea, which, let it be announced, will be strictly punished.

"In accordance with this license some ships were sent out first to spy out convenient places. One of these was taken last winter by the Spanish and the people were badly treated. This spring a Captain Newport was sent to that place with about one hundred fifty men on behalf of the first company, called the southern company. These people were under the command of Edward Maria Wingfield, and were to prepare everything for the next voyage in which entire households would be brought there, with women and children. This group arrived satisfactorily and set their people ashore by a large, beautiful river, which place is as yet unnamed. They drove off a few Indians and put up a three-sided fort. Thereabout they planted a part of a hectare of land to maize, on which they could live for a long time. The river is very full of fish; they found many grapevines high in the trees as thick as a man's waist. They found much mountain crystal in the mountains, and brought from there several minerals, but as yet nothing of value has been found in them. Leaving a small ship and about a hundred men or more, Captain Newport returned, being about five weeks on the way, and loaded his ship with clapboards and other things which they thought might be rare there, in order to make a trial of everything.

"The main promoter of this colony died in June in England, namely, Sir John Popham, Chief Justice of England and Councilor, a courageous, intelligent man of high reputation, and he is much lamented."

At this point Van Meteren's chronicle is interrupted by brief mention of the first voyage of Henry Hudson in search of a northeast passage. He then goes on to describe preparations being made by Willem Usselinx for the establishment of a Dutch West India Company.

In his collection of documents relating to the history of Virginia, Alexander Brown states that Samuel Purchas first published the Virginia patent in abstracted form in 1625.[25] Robert A. Brock confirms this in his chapter in *Narrative and Critical History of America*.[26] Van Meteren's abstract, however, is in many respects so close to the original patent in both form and content as to admit of no doubt that it was based upon the original letters patent or some document closely related to them. It is noteworthy that in listing the names which appear at the beginning of the letters patent, Van Meteren gives them in the same order as the original document. Likewise, when he mentions Bristol, Exeter, and Plymouth they are in the same order as in the original patent. Furthermore, a reading of Van Meteren's abstract in conjunction with the complete document reveals that with but one exception he followed the order of the provisions although he eliminated the legalistic redundancies and some of the later provisions which did not pertain specifically to settlement of Virginia. He did lift a provision for the free passage of goods in Virginia Company ships from paragraph fourteen and place it with material from paragraph eleven. Otherwise his sequence of provisions follows that of the original perfectly.

It is apparent, therefore, that Van Meteren's information on the letters patent did not come out of mere street conversation, and his early news of Virginia also proves to be well founded. He mentions the reconnaissance voyages which followed the licensing of the Virginia enterprise. In August 1606 Henry Challons took a ship out to Virginia, and in October Captains Hanham and Pring followed. Challons was taken by the Spaniards, and is presumably the one referred to by Van Meteren. Much more information has survived relating to Captain Newport's voyage of "this spring" as noted by Van Meteren. His estimate of one hundred and fifty men is quite close if the crew are counted, for actually one hundred forty-two men sailed in the *Susan Constant*, the *God-Speed*, and the *Discovery* when they left England early in January 1607, and Wingfield became the group's leader when he was chosen president by the other council members upon their arrival in Virginia.

Van Meteren's statement that the place at which the settlers in Virginia arrived was fruitful but not yet named indicates that he had access to information from among those who did not like the name "Jamestown" given to the settlement, for that was the name decided upon very early by the settlers.[27] In a letter of August 18, 1607, Dudley Carleton, the English diplomat, wrote to John Chamberlain of Newport's return from Virginia, having left the settlers "in an Island in the midst of a great river 120 miles into the land." He continued, "They write much commendations of the aire and the commodities of it: but silver and golde have they none, and they can not yet be at peace with the inhabitants of the countrie. They have built a small towne which they call James-towne, and so they date their letters. But the towne me thinks hath no graceful name . . ."[28] Then he added in a postscript: "Mr. Porie [Pory] tells me of a name given by a Dutchman who wrote to him in Latin from the new towne in Virginia, Jacopolis, and Mr. Warner hath a letter from Mr. George Percie who names their towne James-fort which we like best of all the rest . . ."[29] The discontent with the name of the settlement appears to have extended to English and Dutch in both Virginia and London.

The presence of a Dutchman in Virginia suggests a very early interest in the English settlement, as, indeed does Van Meteren's publication of the Virginia letters patent. Frequent use of the term "Dutchman" to mean German at this time might support the view that John Pory's correspondent was one of the German artisans taken to Virginia to develop metal and glass works, but it seems less likely to have been a German artisan writing to a member of Parliament in Latin about Jamestown than some Dutch observer from the London colony with whom Pory could have had an acquaintance. In view of the plans of Willem Usselinx, it would have been most natural for a Dutchman to have sought this opportunity to witness the establishment of the Virginia colony.

Van Meteren's remarks on the abundance of fish and forest products correspond to other early reports on Virginia. His concern for minerals reflects a keen interest ever in the minds of the company's adventurers, as is shown in a letter written by Sir Thomas Smith, treasurer of the Virginia Company, to Salisbury, the lord treasurer, during the summer of 1607 when Newport was preparing to make another voyage to Virginia. Here Smith recommended Newport's using a "nymble pynnace" so the voyages to Virginia and back could be made quickly in order to speed up news concerning ore which was being tested in Virginia.[30] But other products were of interest also, and the "clapboards and other things" which Van Meteren records in the first Virginia cargo correspond to descriptions of this and later cargoes given in subsequent publications of the colony.[31] Van Meteren's figure of about one hundred colonists left in Virginia is also substantiated by later historians.[32]

The colony was planted, and this time there would be no Spanish Armada to divert England from keeping it supplied until its roots were firm in the American soil. Captain Newport's major function was to shuttle between England and Virginia, bringing back samples of American commodities, and taking out more settlers to the New World. The *Susan Constant* arrived in England on its first eastbound journey on June 22, 1607, and preparations were begun at once for the return voyage to Virginia. Settlers were assembled, and Van Meteren recorded: "The English company of Virginia in October sent two ships to that place with about two hundred men, with the intention of sending more people the year following, including some women and children, to live there according to the license previously mentioned."

The two ships referred to here were under the command of Captains Newport and Francis Nelson. Newport arrived in Virginia on January 8, 1608, but Nelson was delayed by storms, stopped in the West Indies, and did not show up in Jamestown until mid-April. The accuracy of Van Meteren's estimate of the number of colonists who sailed in this "first supply" may be questioned, for neither contemporary nor later historians placed it as high as two hundred.[33] Indeed, Van Meteren himself reduced the estimate later to "about eighty men" who were landed in Virginia.[34] Nevertheless, what must have been most important to him and to those who hoped to carry the war to Spain in America was the fact that the colony was going forward without opposition from the Crown despite complaints from Spain.

The Dutch not only cheered the English on, but apparently offered their assistance also, arousing fear in the heart of Don Pedro de Zuñiga that Virginia was a front for Dutch activities against Spain. He wrote to his king on January 24, 1607, that "all this is seeking a way to encourage the rebels against your Majesty." [35] He reported that Noel de Caron, the Dutch ambassador to England, had suggested that it was necessary for the Dutch to assist the English in Virginia or the latter would be totally ruined there, but the idea was dropped when James did not receive it well.[36]

It was understandably hard for Spain to see the planting in Virginia as anything but an invasion of her American preserve by a nation that had for two generations been moving toward that objective. Zuñiga's sovereign wrote on March 8, 1607, "you will report to me what the English are doing in the matter of Virginia — and if the plan progresses which they contemplated, of sending men there and ships — and thereupon it will be taken into consideration here what steps had best be taken to prevent it." [37]

[33

Zuñiga's view of Virginia was clearly stated on October 5, about the time Captains Newport and Nelson were sailing for Virginia with their colonists, for he wrote to his king "that it is not their intention to plant colonies, but to send out pirates from there, since they do not take women, but only men." [38] When he brought the subject up in an interview with James three days later, James feigned lack of any specific knowledge of Virginia, but agreed that it was probably a very sterile place which would make it useful primarily for piracy. Nevertheless, he held that Englishmen were not violating the 1604 treaty with Spain in going there. James agreed that the Spanish were quite right to punish any Englishmen who molested them in the New World, and he would, he said, get assurance from the Virginia people that they would not harm Spanish possessions. Zuñiga felt that it would be better if James would just put an end to the whole enterprise, but here again James balked. [39]

Meanwhile, since Spain interpreted the Virginia settlement as a violation of the peace, she felt justified in holding prisoners taken off ships en route to or from America. But this interpretation was being gently challenged by Salisbury in negotiations for release of such prisoners with Zuñiga in London. [40] Here were signs of firmness to cheer Spain-haters, yet in these days late in 1607 England was less gently moving the Dutch toward the truce with Spain. There was a danger, however, in exerting too much pressure on the Dutch, for they appeared to be drawing closer to France, and if the French became their principal ally against Spain, the payment of substantial sums of money which the Netherlands owed England might be impeded. When Spain came close to meeting the demands of the Netherlands for complete independence, Winwood and Spencer felt the Dutch could not in honor hold out for more. They hoped the Netherlands would accept the treaty, and "wished them to do it the sooner the better." [41]

If the truce was not signed, it seemed likely that the West India Company of Willem Usselinx would shortly appear on the American scene, for the 1607 charter granted to the company the exclusive right of trade in America from the Strait of Magellan to Newfoundland as well in Africa from Cape Verde to the Cape of Good Hope. The company had the backing of Holland and Zeeland, the two most powerful and commercially active states of the Netherlands, and it also had the support of the most knowledgeable geographers in the Low Countries, Jan Huygen van Linschoten, François Francken, and Petrus Plancius. The company and the States-General were each to supply sixteen ships for the company's use, the taking of prizes at sea was encouraged by the charter, and the company was to be free to build forts, to wage war, and to settle colonies as it saw fit.[42]

In comparison the Virginia Company may well have seemed a weak effort, and the English understandably kept a wary eye on this competitor. Among other materials pertaining to events of 1607 in the Public Record Office is to be found the cover to the English translation of the charter of the Dutch company;[43] there can be no doubt that the entire document was in hand in 1607.

Although the Dutch West India Company may have appeared as a threat to English Virginia, it was much more of a danger to Spain in America, for it was anti-Spanish in concept. It was, in fact, used as a part of the argument of the Dutch war party which supported peace only if religious and other freedoms for the southern provinces were granted, something Spain could not possibly do. The continuation of the war was advocated as the only honorable course open to the Dutch by pamphleteers who flooded the Netherlands with their writings in 1608, and the establishment of the company in America was considered an essential stratagem if Spain was to be defeated decisively. A group of these pamphlets were collected and sold by a bookseller under the title *Den Nederlantschen Bye-Korf*.[44] The fact that a number of them appeared in more than one issue suggests that they were very popular.

As the peace negotiations progressed, Emanuel Van Meteren reported them in an appendix to the 1608 edition of his *History*. His eyes were not entirely on his homeland, however, for as news came in from Virginia with the return of Captain Newport, he incorporated this note into the appendix:

"A certain Captain Newport returned to England, having been gone to a part of the colony of Virginia. He was five weeks en route, and landed about eighty men there. Another ship that was with him going over was not yet there six months ago, but has arrived since. It is a good land full of vineyards, with abundance of fruit and good people. He brought along a son of the king there as a hostage. This captain has gone back there about the middle of July." [45]

There was little else of an encouraging nature that Van Meteren could have reported to those eager for news from Virginia. Dissension and want were the order there. Council President Edward Maria Wingfield returned to England with Newport, a fact conveniently overlooked by Van Meteren, and the news he brought included a tale of something akin to rebellion, and a report of the execution of its chief fomenter, Captain Kendall. Wingfield was also forced to defend himself to the London Council of Virginia against charges of wanting to desert the colony, of misappropriation of supplies, of being an atheist and in the service of Spain.[46] Wingfield's defense brought into some prominence the activities of Captain John Smith, a member of the Council in Virginia, not only as an accuser of the president, but also as an energetic explorer and supplier of food for the settlers.[47]

It is impossible to know with certainty whether Van Meteren was aware of all these difficulties, but it seems likely that one who had the correct information on the time required for Newport's return, who was informed of the temporary disappearance and return of Captain Nelson and the *Phoenix*,[48] and who was able to announce the company's plans for the following year was also well aware of the problems besetting the colony.

Van Meteren's omission from his narrative of all that was unpleasant is understandable as a natural disinclination to give comfort to the enemy, to make it appear that Spain could wipe out the little colony with the slightest effort. And, indeed, Spain was apparently preparing to make such an effort in 1608, for Ambassador Cornwallis reported from Madrid on April 19 that twelve galleons were being built "for the guarding of the Coast of the West Indies." [49] That coast can only have meant Virginia to Cornwallis, for on May 17 he worried, "My hope is his Majesties Subjects that are in Virginia shall not be uncared for, to whom I suspect this Sommar there will be given some Alarum." [50] The ambassador could only guess what actions the Spaniards had in mind, but he was aware that Virginia was a subject worthy of consideration by the Spanish Council of the Indies late in June 1608. [51] There was every reason to believe that Spain opposed an English settlement so close to her own American possessions just as much as she opposed Dutch trade in Spanish America. If the Spanish negotiators could not stand off the Dutch insistence on the freedom to trade in America, Spanish ships might encounter less opposition from the frail settlement in Virginia.

The English colony might in fact have been quickly disposed of by Spain, had she not valued England's friendship at this time in her struggle with the Dutch. According to John Ogle, a soldier of long experience in the Low Countries, the Dutch had one hundred eighty ships in the East and West Indies, [52] enough to foretell the doom of Spain in both hemispheres. While Spain made a show of readiness to continue the war, and negotiated an alliance with France, she sought the help of James in bringing the Dutch to a truce. Winwood and Spencer, England's representatives at the peace talks, did their best, and by November 6 measured their progress with satisfaction. "Our patience and indeavours thus far have advanced the business that six of the provinces are . . . resolved to enter into a treaty of truce." [53] Only Zeeland held out for greater clarity in Spain's recognition of the absolute independence of the United Provinces.

Winwood and Spencer did not represent all of England, however, and they heard from dissenters who saw no need to push the Dutch, their old allies, into a truce with Spain. Sir Henry Neville lamented this enthusiasm for peace, and hoped for a resumption of the old alliance as he wrote to Winwood, "I profess that I hold their [the Dutch] Interest and ours so nearly conjoyned . . . and would as willingly contribute even beyond all proportion of my Meanes and cooperate as seriously with my

Voice and best Endeavour in Parliament to enable the King to yield them a real assistance, as I would for the pacifying of Ireland." [54] John More saw a remedy against the Franco-Spanish alliance "by taking the present Occasion . . . to stryke close Hands with the States . . . to assure them wholly to our selves." [55]

Despite the vehemence of such men in England and the energy of Usselinx and others of like mind in the Netherlands, despite the prayer of Sir Ferdinando Gorges that "we repent not too late our too soone concluding of peace," England and the Netherlands found peace with Spain the most desirable course. By the closing weeks of 1608 it was clear that a truce for twelve years would be signed, and as Emanuel van Meteren sent the last pages of his appendix to the 1608 edition to press, he recorded there the negotiations that brought to a pause the war that was nearly as old as he was.

The terms of the truce were wonderfully ambiguous with reference to Dutch trade in the Indies, and actually prohibited nothing. It was obvious, however, that the Dutch West India Company, so clearly designed to exploit Spanish commerce in America, could not be permitted to begin its work, and it did not, in fact, begin to function until the truce expired in 1621.

England received little thanks for its help in bringing about the truce, for the temporary demise of the Dutch West India Company removed only one of the threats to Spain in the New World; in the Spanish view the Virginia Company was hardly less aggressive. Spain's suspicion of England was reflected in the fact that James, even while he was working to achieve a peace acceptable to Spain, had been reviled in that country for supposedly holding the Dutch to their hard terms. [56]

The new order of peace seemed to have less reason for existence than the old struggle in which England and the Netherlands had stood together. This appeared especially true to those who looked toward Virginia. In his *True Relation of Such Occurrences . . . as Hath Hapned at Virgina*, the only book that described Virginia before the end of 1608, Captain John Smith spoke of Spain as the enemy of that colony. He spoke also of the internal difficulties there which rendered the colony ineffective in its first years. Yet food shortages, difficulties with the Indians and with each other, did not bring despair to him, and he hoped to stimulate interest among Englishmen in building upon the beginnings of stability which he claimed to have given the colony. He reported with optimism "We now remaining being in good health, all our men wel contented, free from mutinies, in love one with another, and as we hope in a continual peace with the Indians, where we doubt not but by God's gracious assistance, and the adventurers willing minds, and speedie furtherance to so honorable an action in after times, to see our Nation enjoy a Country, not onely exceeding pleasant for habitation, but also very profitable for commerce in general, no doubt pleasing to almightie God, honourable to our gracious Soveraigne, and commodious generally to the whole Kingdome." [57]

These were hopeful words to counter the reports of dissension and fear of Spanish interference in Virginia. They promised Emanuel van Meteren and his countrymen that with time and effort a bulwark against Spain could be built in the New World to limit Spanish expansion there, even as it had been limited in Europe.

DUTCH AND ENGLISH VOYAGES

THE confidence in the ultimate success of Virginia displayed by Captain John Smith was not shared by the company's London directors. They showed, rather, an air of desperation when in October of 1608 they sent Captain Newport back to Virginia with the charge that he return to England bearing a lump of gold, news of a northwest passage, or survivors of Raleigh's lost colony. Newport was also induced to promise that he would bring back a cargo worth 2000 pounds. If he failed in these pledges the Virginia Company was going to abandon the colony.

Yet despite this demand for reassurance, there was an appreciation of the fact that a major part of Virginia's trouble lay in its unwieldy government, which had caused wrangling and suspicion among the councilors in Virginia. A new charter providing for a single civil and military authority was drawn up, therefore, and, after approval by both the councilors of the company and the king, became effective on May 23, 1609. The first governor was Thomas West, Lord Delaware; his lieutenant governor was Sir Thomas Gates, who had been a soldier in the Netherlands since 1604. Gates was granted a year's leave of absence by the States-General to undertake the settling of a new group of colonists in Virginia,[1] indicating a continued interest in the new colony on the part of the Dutch.

Now did Virginia begin to make an impression on England, for London was assaulted by an aggressive campaign to recruit settlers — a campaign in which missionary zeal was much in evidence. Sermons and pamphlets carried the Puritan message that it was not just the opportunity awaiting Englishmen in Virginia that ought to claim their attention, but the duty which English Christians had to go there and minister to the savage heathen who lived in darkness without the light of the Christian faith.

On April 25, a month before the new charter was formally granted, William Symonds preached a sermon to a group of future Virginia colonists. The lesson was from Genesis 12:1–3, "For the Lord had said unto Abram, get thee out of thy Countrey, and from thy kindred, and from thy fathers house, unto a land that I will shew thee. And I will make thee a great nation . . ." [2] There was no doubt or desperation here, only the clear call to duty, for "the Lord that called Abraham into another Countrey doeth also by the same holy hand, call you to goe and carry the Gospell to a Nation that never heard of Christ." [3] The many doubters of the enterprise who infested London were disposed of as the droppings of "some Anabaptist Spicery," or the hatchings "of some popish egge." [4] The preacher was equally impatient with mere lethargy, particularly "the snorting idleness of the ministry" which "rather choose to mind unprofitable questions at home, then gaining soules abroad." [5]

The Reverend Mr. Symonds did not leave the appeal of economic advantage out of his sermon, for Virginia was represented as a place where England's poor might find hope for a better life. In this he was seconded by Robert Johnson, another minister whose speech to a group of adventurers for Virginia also was printed in 1609. [6] He recognized the necessity of investment and of profit, but he counseled: "look it not be chiefe in your thoughts." [7]

Robert Gray too gave London a sermon on the spiritual and economic value of this enterprise "which may either augment your glorie, or increase your wealth, or purchase your eternity." [8] Here was no patience with wealthy men who let their money out to usury or employed it in speculation when it could be used to convert natives in America to England's religion. The same theme fell on the ears of those who heard Daniel Price at Paul's Cross on May 28, 1609, just five days after the new charter was issued. From Acts 9:4, "Saul, Saul, why persecutest thou me?" Price led his hearers through the gloom of sin that clouded their lives in England to the brink of hope where they might see that Virginia was the means to "receive an unspeakable blessing, for they that turne manie to righteousnesse, shall shine as the starres for ever and ever." [9] After he had listed the drunkards, the swearers, and the loose-living Englishmen as persecutors equal to Saul, he added, "If there be any that have opposed any action intended to the glory of God, and the saving of soules . . . let him know that he is a persecutor, and an adversary of Christ." [10]

These sounds of the seventeenth century did not entirely drown those of the sixteenth, for the more materialistic interest in the New World which had been characteristic of the Elizabethan period was reflected in Richard Hakluyt's translation of De Soto's description of Florida [11] and in Pierre Erondelle's translation of chapters from Lescarbot's *New France*. [12] These were rather tired recitations of the merits of the regions lying to the south and north of Virginia, but they too were surely the result of the excitement that was sweeping through London in the spring of 1609.

This new spirit of enterprise and missionary zeal was not lost upon the Spanish ambassador, Zuñiga, who saw in it a continuation of Anglo-Dutch hostility to Spain. On March 5, 1609, he wrote to Philip III, advising him that Sir Thomas Gates, lately a soldier among the rebels in the Netherlands, was taking four to five hundred men and one hundred women to Virginia, with Lord Delaware and seven hundred more settlers to follow shortly. [13] Zuñiga felt that his efforts to put a stop to the entire project constituted a service to his religion and his country. [14] He reported, in particular, that he was in close touch with the Baron of Arundell, who offered his services as a spy upon the English in Virginia. A month later the ambassador wrote that Gates was planning an even larger force, "since they now expect those whom the Rebels will send there." [15]

The term "rebels" was regularly used by Zuñiga to apply to the

Dutch, and it appears that there may have been some justification for his fear that the Dutch were partners in the Virginia undertaking. In May 1609 Captain Thomas Holcroft was sent by the councilors in London to the Netherlands with a letter describing the Virginia colony in order to recruit colonists from among the English troops still in the Low Countries. The letter went further than this, however, stating that "we desire to Invite unto us and our Company so many of his Majesty's subjects or others that be willing or desirous to join . . . in this present supply." [16] The "others" in this instance could only be Dutch. Captain Holcroft's letter also appeared to base the need for more colonists in part on military necessity, for the Virginia population as then constituted was said to be "too few . . . to defend themselves against an enemy that daily threatens." [17]

Emanuel van Meteren must have watched these preparations for the revitalizing of Virginia with the greatest interest; there were other developments to follow also. While the Council of Virginia was forging its new charter in the spring of 1609, an English sea captain named Henry Hudson sailed from Holland on a voyage that at first appeared to have no significance for Virginia. Hudson had made two voyages in search of a northeast passage for English interests and was now in the employ of the Dutch East India Company to try again to gain access to the East Indies over this route. It is entirely possible that Van Meteren was the person who put the Dutch merchants in touch with Hudson, for as we have seen he had earlier rendered a similar service.[18] Furthermore, in his early references to Hudson, he gives him the Christian name "Thomas," which name is also used in some of the earliest Dutch documents relating to the voyage.[19] And when the voyage was completed, with Hudson stopping in England and being held there by English authorities, it was Emanuel van Meteren who received an account of the voyage and published it in the edition of his history which appeared in 1610, this being the first published account of the Dutch penetration of Virginia.[20] A translation follows: [21]

"We have said in the preceding book that the directors of the East In-   [43 dia Company had sent, in the month of March last past, in order to seek a passage to China by the northwest or northeast, a brave English pilot named Henry Hudson, with a well-provided fly-boat, and about eighteen or twenty men, some English and some Dutch. This Henry Hudson sailed from Texel on the 6th of April 1609, and doubled the cape of Norway on the 5th of May. He laid his course toward Nova Zembla, along the northern coast, but found the sea as full of ice there as he had found it the previous year. Whereupon, owing to the cold which some who had been in the East Indies could not stand, the English and Dutch fell into dispute among themselves. Consequently the master, Hudson, gave them their choice between two things. The first of these was to go to the coast of America in the fortieth degree of latitude. He had become interested in this through letters and maps which a certain Captain Smith had sent him from Virginia, and on which was shown a sea by which he might circumnavigate their [the English] southern colony from the north, and from there pass into a western sea. If this had been true, which experience up to the present time has shown to the contrary, it would have been a very advantageous and short route to sail to the Indies.

"The other proposition was to search for the passage by Davis Strait, to which at least they generally agreed. On the fourteenth they set sail and with favorable winds arrived at the isle of Faroe the last of May, stopping there only twenty-four hours to take on fresh water. Leaving there they reached the coast of New France on the eighteenth of July in the latitude of forty-four [degrees] where they were obliged to make a stop to replace their foremast which they had lost, and where they obtained and rigged one.

"They found this a good place for catching codfish and also for carrying on a traffic for good skins and furs which they could obtain for mere trifles, but the sailors behaved very badly toward the people of the country, taking things by force which was the cause of difficulties between them. The English, thinking they would be overpowered and worsted, were afraid to enter further into the country, so they sailed from there on

44]

the twenty-sixth of July and continued at sea until the third of August, when they approached land in the latitude of forty-two degrees. From there they sailed again until the twelfth of August, when they again approached the land at the latitude of thirty-seven and three quarters degrees, and kept their course along it until they reached the latitude of forty and three quarters where they found a good entrance between two headlands.

"Here they entered on the twelfth of September and discovered as beautiful a river as could be found, very large and deep, with good anchorage on both shores. They ascended it with their large vessel as high as forty-two degrees and forty minutes, and went still higher with the ship's boat. At the entrance to the river they found the natives very brave and warlike, but inland, and up to the highest point of the river, they found them friendly and civil, having an abundance of skins and furs such as marten and foxes, and many other commodities, birds, fruits and even white and blue grapes. They treated these people very civilly and brought away a little of whatever they found among them. After they had gone about fifty leagues up the river they returned on the fourth of October, and again put to sea. More could have been accomplished there if there had been good feeling among the sailors, and had not the want of provisions hindered them.

"At sea a consultation was held at which there was a difference of opinion. The mate, who was a Dutchman, thought they ought to go and winter in Newfoundland, and seek for the northwest passage through Davis Strait. The master, Hudson, was opposed to this. He feared his crew would mutiny because at times they had boldly menaced him, and also because they would be completely overcome by the cold of winter and be obliged after all to return with many of the crew weak and sickly. No one, however, spoke of returning home to Holland, which gave the master further cause for suspicion. Consequently he proposed that they should go and winter in Ireland, to which they all agreed, and at length they arrived on November 7 at Dartmouth in England.

"From this place they sent an account of their voyage to their masters   [45 in Holland, proposing to go in search of a passage to the northwest if they were furnished with fifteen hundred guilders in money to buy provisions, in addition to their wages and what they had in the ship. He [Hudson] wished to have some six or seven of his crew changed, making the number up to twenty men, etc., and to sail from Dartmouth about the first of March in order to be in the northwest by the end of that month. He hoped to pass the month of April and half of May in killing whales and other animals in the neighborhood of the isle of Panar, and from there to go toward the northwest and remain there till the middle of September. He then proposed to return again by the northeast of Scotland to Holland.

"Thus was the voyage finished, but before the directors could be informed of their arrival in England a long time elapsed due to contrary winds. At last they sent orders for the ship and crew to return at once to Holland, and when this was about to be done, the master, Henry Hudson, was ordered by the [English] authorities not to depart, but to remain and do service for his own country, which was also required of the other Englishmen on the ship. Many, however, thought it very strange that the masters, who had been sent out for the common benefit of all kinds of navigation, should not be permitted to return in order to render an account and make a report of their doings and affairs to their employers. This took place in January 1610. It was supposed that the English wished to send the same persons with some vessels to Virginia to explore further the before mentioned river."

There is a tone of disillusionment in Van Meteren's remark that many thought it strange that Hudson and his men, whose navigation was to be of "common benefit," were not permitted to return home to Holland, whence they had begun. He was still thinking of Anglo-Dutch cooperation as he had known it in Elizabeth's time, when Englishmen and Dutchmen shared a war against Spain for common benefit. He was getting out of touch with his own people too, for despite the mixed crew, and the fact that Smith's maps and the journals of Captain Weymouth

had been discussed by Hudson and Petrus Plancius, the very knowledgeable adviser to the Dutch East India Company,[22] this was a Dutch voyage, an attempt to find a good route across America to the East Indies, where Dutch merchants, now well established, were shortly to show increasing hostility toward English penetration of their commercial preserve. It is doubtful that they would have shared such a passage with the English any more than necessity demanded if one had been discovered.

While Van Meteren's informant appears to have correctly described the choices Hudson offered his crew when he gave up on the northeast passage, he does not spell out the whole reason why Hudson selected the North American coast at forty degrees north latitude and Davis Strait as alternatives. Hudson's hopes for success at forty degrees appear to have been based on the knowledge he had of the voyages of Captain Weymouth and Captain John Smith. Weymouth had sailed along the coast from north to south to about forty-one degrees thirty minutes in 1605, and Smith had gone northward to about thirty-eight degrees, leaving the area in between unexplored.[23] Hudson and Plancius had studied the possibility of exploring this area before Hudson's departure, but it was not the only opportunity they saw for finding a passage through North America. Hudson believed strongly in the possibility of a passage southward from Lumley's inlet which was to be reached through Davis Strait. This passage was believed to lead southward along the western side of Virginia.[24] While Hudson's instructions did not call for the voyage to America, once it was made the rapidity with which further voyages from the Netherlands followed proves an abundance of interest in the North American coast on the part of the Dutch at that time.

Once again, Van Meteren gives no clue to the source of his account of Hudson's voyage. There is little positive evidence to support the view that it was Hudson himself,[25] yet it is very probable that it was someone in authority on the *Half Moon*, for precision in the matter of dates and degrees of latitude indicates that the information came not from memory, but from a log or journal. In a crew of eighteen or twenty men it is unlikely that many such written records would be kept. The journal kept by Robert Juet, an Englishman sailing with Hudson, is not directly related to Van Meteren's account, so it is probable that Van Meteren's narrative came from Hudson or the mate who was a Dutchman.

As history, Van Meteren's version of Hudson's voyage has no serious shortcomings. He begins with an error by stating that he had noted in the previous book that the Hudson voyage was under way, for no mention of the departure is to be found there. He also is somewhat loose in his interpretation of the Dutch East India Company's orders to Hudson when he says that Hudson was sent "to seek a passage to China by the northwest or northeast," since his instructions called for a voyage northeast and north only.[26] This loose interpretation of the instructions was due, no doubt, to Van Meteren's greater familiarity with the voyage itself than with the wording of the orders. For the crucial period between May 5 and May 14, 1609, when Hudson determined that he could not sail further eastward, and gave his crew a choice of two alternatives on the North American coast, we have no source but Van Meteren, yet it seems a plausible method of decision-making for Hudson: he apparently had a crew with mutinous tendencies, and he gave them a similar choice later when it was decided to leave North America for Ireland.

Concerning the landfall on the North American mainland there is substantial agreement among Van Meteren, Robert Juet,[27] and Joannes De Laet,[28] who wrote fifteen years later and had Hudson's journal before him. All place the landfall in the vicinity of forty-four degrees; all comment on the activity of Frenchmen who were trading with the Indians there. Juet and Van Meteren both report on the necessity of cutting timber for a foremast there and on the difficulties with the natives, although Juet does not leave room for doubt that the Indians were at fault.[29] The next landfall, which Van Meteren places at forty-two degrees, is set by De Laet and Juet at forty-one degrees forty-three minutes and forty-one degrees forty-five minutes respectively. There is a difference of opinion regarding the next landfall as the three authors report Hudson's voyage southward. Whereas Van Meteren has the *Half Moon* making land at thirty-seven and three quarters degrees, on August 12, Juet reports no land until August 17, and then at thirty-seven degrees twenty-six minutes, "the entrance into the Kings River in Virginia, where our English-men are." [30] De Laet sets the landfall at thirty-seven degrees fifteen minutes, gives no date, and names the place Dry Cape. [31]

Neither Van Meteren nor De Laet reports any further sailing southward, but Juet gives a daily account of a continuing voyage in that direction, reporting latitude as low as thirty-five degrees forty-one minutes on August 24. The *Half Moon* then turned north and both Juet and Van Meteren record September 12 as the date Hudson turned into the river that was to bear his name. All three authors give a latitude between forty and forty-one degrees as the position of the ship in the days immediately preceding the ascent of the river. De Laet and Van Meteren agree that the ship sailed up the river to nearly forty-three degrees, and while Juet gives no terminal latitude, he joins them in reporting that some of the ship's boats went beyond into more shallow waters of the river. All three narratives agree about the fruitfulness of the land along the river, and the friendliness of the Indians in the up-river country. Van Meteren contrasted the behavior of the inland natives with that of the natives at the mouth of the river, but his comment did not reveal the extent of the hostility of the latter, for one Englishman, John Colman, was killed and two others wounded in a skirmish with a group of natives at a place they named Colman's Point. [32]

The controversy over where to spend the winter, the return home, and the plans made by Hudson for a subsequent voyage on behalf of the East India Company are not recorded by Juet and De Laet, nor indeed is the fact of Hudson's internment in England. In gathering these final details, Van Meteren was obviously not writing from a journal, but was reporting plans described to him by someone close to Hudson, if not Hudson himself. He appears to have misunderstood the name of the island where Hudson proposed to take whales, for maps and descriptions of the northern regions from this period do not identify an island of Panar.

Thus did Emanuel van Meteren chronicle the beginnings of Dutch enterprise in North America. A Dutch ship and an English captain, Dutch sponsors and English maps, a mixed crew born of the old friendship, but [49 restless and threatening, these were the harbingers of New Netherland. This voyage was not designed to molest the Spaniard, for it was rather an extension of the customary route to Newfoundland, an area where it was the French who had great ambitions. It was, in fact, an invasion of Virginia. Its motive presaged the Anglo-Dutch competition of the seventeenth century, even if its equipment was a holdover from the sixteenth. The Dutch quickly realized that the Hudson River [33] could not lead them to the Pacific Ocean, but with their talent for recognizing trade opportunities, they saw here an area of rich commercial potential. Hudson's inability to report in person did not prevent the news of his discovery from reaching Amsterdam, and in London Van Meteren was quick to share it with the world.

Englishmen were well aware of the commercial propensities of the Dutch, for in 1609 Sir Thomas Overbury, the poet and court personality, wrote, "There belong to that State 20,000 Vessels of all sorts," and he added that if they ever became enemies of the English they would be able "to give us the Law at Sea, and eat us out of all trade." [34] Sir Ralph Winwood was equally realistic about the potentialities of Dutch overseas commerce as he observed that the Dutch were preparing to plant a settlement in the East Indies somewhat after the pattern of Virginia. "The Company of the East Indies," he wrote, "do now send forth into those parts nine Shipps which attend the Wind at the Texell. The States have a purpose to cause those places which they hold, to be inhabited by their own People: Upon which Reason they send with this Fleet many Women and by Commission appoint a Governor there." [35]

These observations were not necessarily unfriendly in tone. They reflected a normal concern for England's comparative weakness in maritime commerce, and perhaps some jealousy, but they do not suggest that the English intended to undermine Dutch commerce. James I, however, did openly assault the foundations of Dutch maritime strength, shattering any notion that the Dutch may have had in this first year of peace that the old alliance still existed. On May 16, 1609, James issued a proclamation by which he proposed to bring an end to the freedom of Dutch fishermen to take fish in the coastal waters of the British Isles. As early as 1295 Hollanders and Zeelanders had been granted the right to fish freely there by English monarchs. Subsequent renewals of these treaties had confirmed the privilege until Dutch fishing in British waters was accepted, not merely as a right, but as a major factor in the Dutch economy. James's statement that "our express pleasure is that . . . no Person of what Nation or Quality soever, be permitted to fish upon any of our Coasts and Seas of Great Britain, Ireland and the rest of the Isles adjacent, until they have orderly obtain'd Licenses from us" [36] raised visions of economic problems of major importance to the Dutch, for the herring that came from these waters were carried to the Baltic countries to be exchanged for grain to feed the Dutch people and for timber and hemp, which were the sinews of the Dutch merchant fleet. The fishing trade stimulated the salt trade which took Dutch ships to Spain, Portugal, France, and Venezuela. It schooled sailors who would eventually graduate to the more distant voyages of the East India Company's ships.

Herring, then, was at the heart of the Dutch maritime trade, and the threat to it in James's proclamation challenged the Dutch to produce their best legal arguments in defense of their ancient privileges — or, from the Dutch point of view, rights. Elias van Oldenbarneveldt, brother of the great statesman and pensionary of Rotterdam, presented the case before an Anglo-Dutch conference called to discuss the fisheries question in May 1610, the arguments having probably been prepared by the famed legalist Hugo Grotius. When this issue was joined with other problems, matters of Continental politics which pointed up the need for Anglo-Dutch harmony, both sides yielded some ground. The Dutch did not push their claim to fishing "rights" in an offensive manner, and James, while maintaining his prerogative to grant licenses for fishing, deferred the enforcement of the proclamation for two years. [37]

Meanwhile, Emanuel van Meteren was setting down more details of the Virginia colony, in words that did not reveal a strong sense of rivalry but rather pointed to a concern for the survival and welfare of the English settlement. When he had finished the narrative of Hudson's voyage, he continued on with an account of Virginia: [38]

"The English company, of which we have written in the 28th book, this year has very earnestly set out to further settlement of their colony. To this end they have obtained more generous privileges and patents from their king. They had settled themselves in a bay called Chessiopoock [Chesapeake] lying at thirty-seven degrees north latitude, where they have built a fort as the beginning of a city which they have named Jamestown after their king.

"In the previous summer they first sent a ship there under Captain Argall to discover a suitable passage because the southern passage by way of the Indies is very dangerous and likely to bring them into conflict with the Spaniards. Therefore they forbade Captain Argall to approach any territories of the king of Spain, and especially [ordered him] to set his course so as to be free of pirates which lie in passages and close to the shore, and leaving the Canary Islands to the east to take a course directly westward as nearly as possible, and thereby explore the winds and ocean currents and note any obstacles that might hinder this northern voyage. Should this route be found, it would bring to the company great security and comfort and would also remove any cause for conflicts and disagreements between them and the Spanish. It would even spare the English half of the expenses which they have had to lay out, and would be especially saving in food and time.

"To this end Captain Argall left Portsmouth on the fifteenth of last May, set his course southwest to thirty degrees, leaving the Canary Islands one hundred miles to the east, then directing his course straight westward, and went no further south. As he came to the longitude of Bermuda he found the wind slight, but nevertheless he arrived in the port in Virginia on July 23.

"In this voyage he found no unfavorable current nor anything else that might make this course to be feared. He made the trip in nine weeks, during two of which he was becalmed. Therefore he believed he could
52] make the voyage in seven weeks, saying that the winds were not so un-

dependable as they were elsewhere, and that the voyage was pleasant and convenient. While they were at sea they caught so many fish that they could have had shiploads of them if they had known how to salt them. It was their misfortune that a man who had the knowledge died on the voyage. However, they did bring [to the colony] some caviar, that is, salted eggs of sturgeon.

"When Captain Argall arrived in Virginia, he found great dissension and division among the English there, and among the commanders also because of their ambition to dominate one another. They were also in great need of food and supplies because they had become lazy and would not work, so that they had almost completely lost heart. Consequently they hoped that the Indians would continue to do business with them and supply them, and they had let pass the time of seeding and all of their provisions were depleted.

"Since they were in an almost despairing situation they were refreshed with the fish which Captain Argall had caught. They betook themselves to fishing and sought to sustain themselves because the Indians, after having seen that the English were increasing in number, held back and would gladly have starved them out and thus been rid of them."

Van Meteren's account of Captain Argall's voyage indicates that he had access to the same information as was used by the Virginia Company in publishing its *True and Sincere Declaration of the Purpose and Ends of the Plantation Begun in Virginia*,[39] issued in 1610. Since Van Meteren's version of the voyage appeared the same year,[40] it would have been possible for him to have used the published pamphlet. Surely he must have known of the *Declaration*, and his own account is in some respects an amplification of it, for he was writing for a Continental audience, not for the London critics of the Virginia Company and the company's investors as the author of the *Declaration* was. For example, Van Meteren was more blunt in his statement of the reason for Captain Argall's voyage, namely, that the continued use of the old southern route to Virginia was likely to bring the English into conflict with the Spaniards. There is no disagreement between the two accounts as to the basic purpose or plan of the voyage, although Van Meteren shows his independence in using the old style in dating it, making his date of departure and arrival ten days later than those found in the *Declaration*. Also, he had Argall turn west at one hundred miles west of the Canary Islands while the *Declaration* said one hundred leagues.

The major differences begin to appear as Van Meteren takes up the final part of the voyage, when Argall's ship reaches Virginia and finds the settlers in a desperate condition. He leaves no doubt of the dissension, division, laziness, and despair which prevailed in the settlement, nor does he try to make excuses. The company's report to the public on this same score understandably attempts to make the best of a bad situation, noting the "rumor of the necessity and distresse our people were found in," [41] but charging that "the noise . . . exceeded the truth." [42] It was useless to deny the troubles in the colony, but the company spokesman was at greater pains in the *Declaration* to explain than to describe them, and attributed the difficulties to "the misgovernment of the Commanders . . . and . . . the Idleness and bestiall slouth of the common sort." [43] According to this version "so soone as Captain Argall arrived among them, whose presence and example gave new assurance of our Cares, and new life to their indeavours, by fishing onely in a few days, they were all recovered, growne hearty, able and ready to undertake every action." [44] The want of food in this land which had been represented as wonderfully fertile was attributed to excessive dependence on the natives for supply, and this "trade to which they trusted betrayed them to loose [*sic*] the opportunity of seedtime . . . for the Naturals withdrew from all commerce and trafficke with them." [45]

This is a somewhat less blunt view than that of Van Meteren, who pictured for his readers a group of lazy colonists unwilling to make the effort to fill their own needs by planting and fishing, and hence faced with the danger of starvation when the Indians who had been providing them with food cut off supplies.

Both of these reports on Captain Argall's voyage identify the correct motives for it, namely, the search for a shorter passage to Virginia and one safe from conflict with the Spaniards, and the wish to find out if a fishing trade could be developed off the coast of Virginia. Argall's crossing, by the route directly westward from the Canaries, required about ten weeks, an improvement over previous westward crossings from England; the fishing proved good; and he had no difficulties with the Spaniards on this route.

But Spain was still to be reckoned with, for as Argall sailed toward the Virginia coast, orders were issued by the Spanish governor of Florida, Pedro de Ybarra, to Captain Francisco Fernandez de Ecija specifying that he was to sail along the North American coast from St. Augustine to forty-four degrees thirty minutes north in search of suitable places for the Spanish government to erect fortifications, and to observe closely what places might already be inhabited by non-Spanish peoples. He was to be especially watchful in the vicinity of thirty-seven degrees thirty minutes because it was believed the English were settled there. He was authorized to attack ships met en route if he thought it prudent to do so.[46]

The *Asuncion de Christo,* carrying twenty-five men, turned its prow northward toward Virginia on June 26, 1609, sailing close to the shore and putting in frequently to gather information from the Indians along the way. The Indians told of an English settlement, and of ships that went back and forth between the colony and England, making it clear that a thriving settlement was already well established near Chesapeake Bay. The Spanish captain decided that if he was to have a look at this colony it must be under false colors, so he masked his vessel as a ship of Amsterdam. In this guise the *Asuncion de Christo* sailed close enough on July 24 and 25 for the crew to see a ship which they believed had been assigned to guard the harbor. This may have been Captain Argall's ship, just recently arrived, and it was sufficient to convince the Spaniards that the English were settled nearby and that their best course of action was to return at once to St. Augustine with the news.[47]

Neither Van Meteren nor any of his contemporaries mentions this ship approaching Jamestown, but the English and Dutch alike were aware that ships from St. Augustine could sail to Jamestown with ease, giving point to Noel de Caron's remark that the English could not survive there without Dutch aid, for the Netherlands had the greater fleet. The mask that the Spanish ship wore bespoke the Spaniard's belief that in Virginia Dutch ships were welcome.

The reputation of Virginia that had filtered through the wilderness to Spanish ears far exceeded reality, but a fleet was on its way to give substance to the rumor of a populous and busy settlement on the James River. The ships that had been prepared as the new Virginia charter was written, and the settlers that had been recruited in the heat of Puritan enthusiasm, were ready for departure by June 1, and a week later the nine vessels set sail for Virginia. The preparations for the voyage and the subsequent adventure were of great interest to Emanuel van Meteren, and following his narrative of Argall's voyage he wrote:

"After Captain Argall departed from England in May, seven ships and two pinnaces were built and prepared in which about five hundred men were to depart for Virginia together with all the things they would need there. The complete command over these, as well as those who were already there, was given to Sir Thomas Gates, a clever and brave man who had long served in the Netherlands and still had a company in Zeeland under his lieutenant. He was to be the absolute leader of this group according to instructions given him, along with George Somers as Admiral and Captain Newport as Vice-Admiral, with other persons able and well qualified. They had sealed orders in which it was determined who should succeed to power in the event of the death of one of them. There were also in this fleet thirty or forty women, and also some stallions and fourteen or fifteen mares with some bulls and cows, although they had high hopes of finding other cattle within six or seven days' travel from the English settlement. They also sent goats and ewes, but no sheep, for the export of wool was forbidden in the interest of the welfare and profit of England. They also sent out other animals, even hogs which already had quickly increased in number.

56]   "It required some time to equip this fleet, and the ships lay off the

coast for a long time, waiting upon one another. They finally set sail from Falmouth on February 18,[48] and in a few days arrived at the latitude of the Canary Islands where they counseled together and decided to go southward to the Tropic of Cancer and then to the west. They also set the policy that if they should be separated by bad weather or lose one another, the Admiral-ship should head for Barvada, an island lying not far to the west of Santo Domingo, and there each ship should wait seven days for the others. When they had gone about one hundred fifty miles under this resolution they found themselves in a great storm on St. James's Day.[49] It lasted forty-eight hours, and it scattered the fleet, many of the ships losing their masts. Three days later four of the ships came together again, but the Admiral-ship was not among them, and since they had a good wind they set their course directly for Virginia without regard for the previous resolution. They arrived at the harbor of Jamestown on August 21. On this route at forty-four degrees south of Virginia they found no current to hinder the voyage to the northwest.[50] A few days after the arrival of these four, three other ships arrived, leaving them with the belief that the Admiral had gone to Barvada Island, although they had no knowledge of it.

"These seven ships landed four hundred men, but no chief or commander, of which almost all were on the Admiral-ship. There was, therefore, no government in the land, because no one wanted to yield to the other. Sir George Percy, brother of the Earl of Northumberland, was highest in rank among those who were there, but nevertheless he had no authority over them.[51] For this reason, some of them, with a few supplies that they were able to get, sailed homeward. When they came near to the coast of Brittany the two ships were dashed against the rocks, from which only one man of the entire company survived.

"Despite this news, the English did not lose hope. Instead they equipped three or four ships to go there [Virginia], with which they sent Lord Delaware as Governor, with abundant provisions and supplies of all kinds, although they did not give up hope that Thomas Gates, together with the others on the Admiral-ship, would have arrived in the meantime. These ships intended to take the most direct and safest route, that of Captain Argall mentioned above. They [the Virginia Company] hold certain that they will still find living in Virginia some of the Englishmen who went out with Sir Walter Raleigh, and that they are to be found fifty miles from the place where the new arrivals have settled, since several indications of this have been found, particularly crosses and other signs carved here and there in the trees.

"It was also planned that in the spring all sorts of artisans should be sent, but only those of the reformed religion, along with four preachers to bring the Indians to the Christian faith. Among the artisans were smiths, carpenters, sail makers, fishermen, coopers, gardeners to plant sugar cane and vineyards, refiners of salt, and jobs of that sort, and also those that were concerned with shipbuilding and everything else necessary to shipping."

Van Meteren apparently wrote this account of the events of Virginia between April and September 1610,[52] and the total impression he leaves is one of undiminished optimism among the directors of the enterprise, despite the misfortunes he describes. These misfortunes were not inconsiderable. Indeed Van Meteren could have been more specific and noted that with the disappearance of the *Sea Venture* three intended leaders of the colony were lost, George Somers and Captain Newport, Admiral and Vice-Admiral of the fleet, as well as the man who was supposed to have been in charge of the colony until Lord Delaware arrived, Thomas Gates. Van Meteren was quite correct, therefore, in stating that there was no government in the land. It is remarkable in this connection that he should completely overlook Virginia's most controversial figure, Captain John Smith, but he is not mentioned at any point in Van Meteren's accounts of the settlement on the James River. In commenting on Sir George Percy's failure to win acceptance of his leadership from the colonists he goes farther than the *Declaration* issued by the Virginia Company.

He also departs from the company's version of the voyage in his account of the preparations for it. He alone gives the number of persons who were to sail at about five hundred, and his narrative is the only source of this early period to note the inclusion of women among the colonists. His report on the plans to raise livestock in Virginia is also unique among the earliest published accounts of this voyage. The exclusion of sheep that he noted is interesting as a prelude to subsequent regulations imposed on aspects of the American colonial economy threatening to harm the economy of the mother country, regulations which had such resounding effects.

In his account of the arrival of seven of the ships at Jamestown, Van Meteren neglects to mention that in addition to the *Sea Venture*, the *Catch* was also missing, and actually was lost at sea. Despite such losses men of this time had faith in the sea, or rather faith in their little ships, far beyond their faith in their fellow men. They took their chances with the Atlantic Ocean to escape the unhappiness they suffered in England, and as Van Meteren noted, in desperation some of them fled from the well-intended authority of Sir George Percy in Virginia only to lose their lives within a few days' sail of England. In reporting this episode, Van Meteren was once more publishing a part of the Virginia story that was not available elsewhere.

His statement of the company's plans for the future again shows that he was in close touch with someone in the Virginia Council, and one feels that he shared their optimism. He even found reason to report favorably on the activities of those merchants who were to settle the northern part of Virginia as he wrote: "In Book 28 we set forth the pattern by which the English were to settle inhabitants and colonies in two places in Virginia. Now those who had undertaken the establishment of settlements farther to the north, at forty-two degrees, left that place [but] have sent ships there each year, and they carry on trade with the Indians and particularly they get rare and exquisite furs, including marten, fox, and such like." [53]

All thought of settling the area that was to become New England had been given up by 1609, and many of the people involved in the original charter licensing the colonization of that area were cooperating in the strengthening of the southern Virginia colony. Yet it is certain that English trade continued along the coast in the vicinity of the Kennebec River where the earlier settlement had stood, and Van Meteren's reference to it adds to the scanty information available on this area between 1606 and 1614, when Captain John Smith explored there.

By the time Van Meteren wrote of these events in Virginia, French, Dutch, English, and Spanish merchants and officials were giving ever-increasing attention to the North American coast between thirty-four and forty-five degrees north latitude. France probed cautiously southward, Dutch merchants eyed trade on Henry Hudson's river, and the English concentrated their strength at Chesapeake Bay, while Spain looked northward along the coast from its Florida stronghold, saw heresy taking root in neighboring Virginia, but as yet dared not break peace in Europe to eradicate it.

STORM AND SURVIVAL

THE summer of 1610 was not a promising one for the Virginia adventurers in London. The murmuring against the colony grew louder as it appeared that the great effort of the previous year had been nullified by the winds of the Atlantic which swept the *Sea Venture* to an unknown fate.

The concern in London over Virginia's debilitating internal problems — disease, dissension, Indian hostility, laziness, and loneliness — was magnified by an awareness that weakness invited attack from the Spaniards, who within living memory of some had wiped out a little group of French Huguenot settlers in Florida, leaving only the statement nailed to a tree that it was "not as Frenchmen, but as Lutherans" [1] that these settlers had been killed. Spain was weaker now, but Madrid was more aware of it than London, and the weakness was more in sea power than in zeal. A Spanish commander might well have been imagined nailing up this epitaph near the ruins of Jamestown: "Not as Englishmen, but as Puritans and pirates." There were certainly those who would have gladly undertaken such a mission, among them the new Spanish ambassador to London, Don Alonso de Velasco, who observed to his king in a tone of recommendation that it would be "very easy to make an end of it altogether by sending out a few ships to finish what might be left in that place, which is so important for pirates." [2]

A thoughtful Englishman must have recognized the challenge to Spain in the recent course of events — and the reasons for a Spaniard's wanting to "make an end" altogether of the colony in the New World [61 before it became firmly established as a base for either piracy or trade which would threaten Spain's dominance in America. The treaty of peace with England and the twelve-year truce with the Dutch were in effect, but the peace was uneasy. For one thing English ships were regularly sailing to the tobacco market in Trinidad, despite the prohibition against trade there. Englishmen and Spaniards alike knew too that in these distant waters illicit trade could not be prevented, and was indeed frequently beneficial. Yet the seaman's choice between illicit trade, which could be overlooked, and acts of piracy, which could not, was more a matter of opportunity than of conscience. As for the Dutch, it was perfectly apparent to anyone who dealt with them that the States-General was not a government, but an association of little governments with no real power to coerce or to restrain the merchants whose far-flung enterprises brought in new wealth that none complained of. Then too the Spanish might well fear a rebirth of the old alliance against them. Hudson's voyage along the North American coast, for example, that reconnaissance of the shores and exploration of rivers along the whole coast that Englishmen called Virginia, had been sponsored by Dutch merchants, but the captain was English and the crew partially so. Was not this the old partnership again, the same that put Dutch flags on English ships in the Caribbean? And was it not strange indeed that in all of James's realm there was no one who could lead the Virginia group save Sir Thomas Gates, a soldier lately in the Netherlands, and actually on leave with permission of the States-General? Good reasons existed for an Englishman to fear Spanish action against a weak Virginia.

There were many among the adventurers who faltered in the face of this danger and Virginia's other problems, but there were others whose passion for the colony drove away fear, or whose motives were such as not to be overcome by fear. On February 21 Lord Delaware, who was soon to leave England to take personal charge of the colony, and others of the Virginia Company heard William Crashaw give such a sermon as to shame a backslider and put steel in the bones of the still faithful investors.[3] This Puritan spokesman gave them Luke 22:33 to ponder:

"But I have praied for thee, that thy faith faile not: therefore when thou art converted strengthen thy brethren."

The message was not subtle. By way of examining Cardinal Bellarmine's treatment of Christ's concern that Peter remain strong in his faith, Crashaw came to the point of his sermon which was the lack of faith in Virginia prevailing among this new set of apostles charged with carrying the message of God to the New World. He discussed the erosion of the company's belief in itself, and the reasons for it. "Wee here see the cause why no more come in to assist this present purpose of plantation in Virginia, even because the greater part of men are unconverted & unsanctified men, and seeke merely the world and themselves, and no further. They make many excuses and devise objections, but the fountaine of all is, because they may not have present profit . . . Tell them of getting XX in the C. Oh how they bite at it, oh how it stirres them! But tell them of planting a Church, or of converting 10,000 soules to God, they are as senseless as stones; they stirre no more than if men spoke of toies and trifles." [4]

It was not merely the recalcitrant investor who felt this zealot's spleen. He addressed himself to all Christian Englishmen by saying "the assistance of this business is a dutie that lies on all men," [5] and the duty was not to the sovereign or to the glory of England. It was a religious duty, for he reasoned, "Either we are not converted or they [the Indians] are not our brethren, or els . . . we being converted must labour their conversion." [6]

In Crashaw's sermon we find reflections of arguments used against Virginia which never showed up in print. He set these negative arguments up, and then shattered them with simple evidence and common sense. The moral argument against taking Virginia from its aboriginal inhabitants was answered in a moral way. The English colonists, Crashaw stated, wanted nothing but what the natives had in overabundance and wished to sell. These were land and commodities. In exchange Englishmen would give commodities useful to the natives and, in addition, the English religion and manners which "will make them richer than we [63 found them." [7] The preacher did not want for evidence to prove the ease of passage to and from Virginia, and the agreeableness of the climate there. To those who held back from supporting so small an enterprise, he gave the example of Rome and its beginnings, and noted "Many greater States (than this is like to prove) had as little or lesse beginnings then this hath." [8] In reply to the undeniable charge that many of the colonists were men of low quality he gave a Puritan's answer, "The basest and worst men trained up in severe discipline, under sharpe lawes, a hard life, and much labour, do prove good members of a Commonwealth." [9] He was not at all alarmed at the reports that came back of the miseries in Virginia, for reporters of such opinions were only those seeking an idle life, and should such miseries indeed exist, they were probably a benefit in the long run, for "were it not good for us if our people were inured to more hardnesse, and brought up under obedience and sharper discipline, and accustomed to lesse daintiness and tenderness then heretofore." [10] He cited the progress of the Dutch during their previous years of trial as proof of his position. And his was a calm voice among those who feared what Spain might do to the little colony in Virginia. He said that Spain would not be so unwise as to break the peace she had with England.

He was less calm, however, in the presence of profit seekers, and he came down hard on those who raised the major objection to Virginia, its insecurity as a field for investment. "If there be any that came in only or principally for profit, or any that would so come in, I wish the latter may never bee in and the former out againe." [11] The main aim of this colony, in William Crashaw's view, was the extension of England's religion to America. Objectors to this idea were either agents of the Devil or papists, and he added theater performers to this company, for the enterprise had been ridiculed from the stage. Players, said Crashaw, disliked the colony "because we resolve to suffer no Idle persons in Virginea, which course if it were taken in England, they know they might turne to new occupations." [12]

64]   This hard-nosed Puritan had a simple formula for success in Virginia:

exclude dissenters in religion and enact a rigid code of laws prescribing the conduct of the colonists, with provision for rigid enforcement. This would make good men of bad ones, and would be a lesson to the English people which would one day guide them to a state of political and moral perfection. With this charge laid upon him, Lord Delaware left London in March and sailed from Plymouth for Virginia in April 1610.

Through the spring and early summer London heard nothing from its colony. Then in September Sir Thomas Gates and Captain Newport appeared in London, victors over the fury of the Atlantic, living testimony that Providence was on the side of the Virginia Company and its servants. The story these men told of the miraculous delivery of the *Sea Venture* and its people, and of their survival on the bewitched island of Bermuda, inspired at least two of England's poets, her best and one of her worst. While Shakespeare plotted *The Tempest*,[13] Richard Rich penned twenty-two stanzas of "honest verse," reducing the entire story to a rough doggerel in this vein:

> It is no fabulous tale,
> nor is it fayned newes:
> For Truth herself is heere arriv'd
> because you should not muse.
> With her, both Gates and Newport come,
> to tell Report doth lye:
> Which did divulge unto the world,
> That they at Sea did dye.[14]

Before the year was out Silvester Jourdain's *A Discovery of the Barmudas* was published, giving the details of the Bermuda adventure as well as a glowing account of the island,[15] and the Virginia Company included the story of the *Sea Venture* and its people in its newest appeal, *A True Declaration of the Estate of the Colonie in Virginia*,[16] published late in 1610 to counter the persisting gloom that was turning people away from the Virginia undertaking.

With London buzzing over the story the survivors told, it is not surprising that Emanuel van Meteren should have made some notes on it as he gathered material for the next edition of his *History*. He was now past seventy-five years of age, yet his narration of this segment of Virginia's history is tolerably accurate, and the following lines translated from it contain a few observations and items of information not met with elsewhere:

"Concerning the English colony or settlement in America which they call Virginia, we have already told in the preceeding book that their last fleet arrived safely except for the Admiral-ship on which were the two noblemen, Gates and Somers, and that three ships under Lord Delaware were sent out in March to set things in order, believing that the ship with these nobles was lost. But this year, in September, Captain Newport returned from there in less than six weeks. He had taken Delaware there, and with him came the nobleman, Sir Thomas Gates, whom people believed to be dead, and who had understood from Lord Delaware that the captaincy that he had in Vlissingen in Zeeland had been given away at the talk of his death. He came back to reclaim it, and told about his adventures, to wit:

"Last year during the storm the Admiral-ship sprang a leak, and had filled with water and they believed that they would be lost. Then they saw Bermuda, an island that the Spaniards believed to be unapproachable because they had suffered many a shipwreck there and had named it Devil's Island. To this island they were miraculously guided, finding a passage between rocks, and they brought the ship in, and ran it aground as high as they could and left it, setting up a marker there also. They landed all the people, at least 120, with all the goods that were in the ship. They had carpenters with all their equipment, and found the island full of all sorts of trees. They found no men or beasts except for many hogs which must have swum ashore from sunken Spanish ships and multiplied there. They also found many birds which were so completely tame that they would fly against one when one was making a fire. There were also many fish there.

"Having found these things, the people began quickly to cut down trees, set up smithies, and build houses, and they finally built two ships from scratch. They lived there thus for forty-two weeks, providing for themselves with such things as they still had with them and with the hogs, birds, and fish. They found salt water among the rocks, which with boiling yielded salt. They found sweet spring water for drinking and cooking. They retrieved some items of iron and other things which they made use of from the wrecks of sunken ships which lay all about. Among them were several families, with women, and two children were born there whom they named Bermuda.

"Since they guessed it was about ten days' voyage to Virginia they built two medium-sized ships to sail there, finding some material in place of pitch and tar with which to make their ships seaworthy. They victualed them with meat of birds, fish, and hogs, and at last after forty-two weeks they set sail, arriving in Virginia among their own people in eleven days. From Virginia Sir George Somers sailed back to Bermuda on June 17 with two ships in order to get hogs and fish and other commodities of which they found some, such as oyster pearls, ambergris, and the like. During all this time they lost only four men, of whom one was a 'Casicke' or son of a king in Virginia who had been in England and who had been killed by an Indian, his own servant. They left some people there, and it seems to be a good place in which to live and prosper.

"Bermuda is an island surrounded by rocks, and with good land in the interior. It is about two or three German miles across, and eight or nine miles long. They [the English] intend to live there and to set up four pieces of artillery at the entrance. They intend to go there with two ships, to live there to get pearls, ambergris, tobacco, etc., and to this end in 1611 they set up a company. Some are of the opinion that there is gold there. This is because several Dutch sailors who have been prisoners in the West Indian galleys, and who fled in a barque, accidentally came to this island in their search for refreshment. Here they found long, thick reeds, growing as large as masts, which they split open, and they made troughs of them, fastening them together to make them longer. In rainy weather for their refreshment they laid these on the ground in the rocks leading to the barque, making the water run from the land and rocks down into their barque. In gathering the water this way, since they had not yet found any fresh water on the island, they found little pieces of gold which the rain had washed loose spilling in with the rainwater. Time will tell if this matter will be investigated further.

"When the people from Bermuda went to Virginia they found great disorder there due to the lack of governors and government. Therefore, in desperation they prepared to leave the country in four ships, and they had already embarked when Lord Delaware arrived to their satisfaction. He remained there, setting things in order. Here and there he made small fortifications further into the country. The leader of the lesser officials went farther inland, and as they penetrated deeper, by water and land, they found it a very good country with all sorts of trees, such as cedar, fir, sassafras, mulberry trees with silkworms, grapevines, game and plenty of fruits, spice and many commodities, so that they were well provided for."

In its essentials, the story Van Meteren tells does not differ from that which has come down to us from other accounts of the voyage. The nine ships that set out for Virginia in June 1609 were not wanting for well-wishers and sermons promising them success in God's work in the New World. But they were wanting in good judgment when the two chief officers of the group, Gates and Somers, sailed in the same ship, the *Sea Venture*, which was commanded by Captain Newport, also commander of the fleet.[17] When the storm came down on them on July 23, this one ship was separated from all the others, and alone it endured a "night of three daies perpetuall horror."[18] The pumps worked continually, but the little ship steadily lost its battle to survive as the sea came into it from every side. The men in the hold stood immersed to their waists as they used their last potable water to drink toasts "taking their last leave one of the other untill their more joyfull and happy meeting, in a more blessed world."[19] Then on the third day the gray sky and raging sea yielded an island to the view of Sir George Somers who stood watch on the poop deck, weak and exhausted like his companions. At the news of land a new energy came to the men of the *Sea Venture*, and they were "carried with a will and desire beyond their strength" [20] to bring the ship to the little known island, the bewitched Bermuda.

In the century that Bermuda had been known to Europeans, it had earned among seamen the name of "Island of the Devils," for winds often tossed ships headlong upon rocks off its coast, shearing their bottoms and sending crew and cargo to a watery grave. The men and women who now came ashore could look for no passing ship to rescue them, for wise captains kept well away. To their surprise, the people of the *Sea Venture* found the island remarkably well provisioned, so that life was easily maintained on the hogs, birds, eggs, fish, and fruits of the island. [21] They did not think of living there permanently, however, and quickly set to work to build two boats which were to take them to Virginia. While this work progressed, life on Bermuda appears to have been much more pleasant than it was in Virginia during the earlier years of its settlement. There is no record of any major discontent among the *Sea Venture*'s passengers while they were on Bermuda; two of them were married during their stay on the island, and two children, a boy and a girl named Bermudas and Bermuda, were born there. [22]

At length, however, a ship, the *Deliverance*, and a pinnace, the *Patience*, were made ready, and on May 10, 1610, the little group set sail for Virginia, arriving at Jamestown two weeks later. Now they found themselves on a continent rather than an island, and wanting desperately for provisions. Famished Virginians rang the church bells to welcome their lost companions to a share in their misery. The government of the place was turned over to Sir Thomas Gates, who surveyed the situation — buildings in a tumbledown condition, having been stripped by the settlers for firewood, supplies exhausted, colonists ill and demoralized — and found the prospects for his group in Virginia poor. He decided to give up the settlement and make for England by way of Newfoundland. There was joy in Jamestown as the settlers contemplated the demise of the little English nation in America. Theirs had been a bitter and a losing struggle. A parting volley was fired, and the four pinnaces bearing some two hundred colonists started on their journey down river toward the Atlantic.

But a cluster of sails greeted them before they reached the coast: three ships with one hundred fifty settlers and a new governor, Lord Delaware. They returned to their deserted settlement to begin another chapter in Virginia's history, and while Sir George Somers volunteered to go back to Bermuda for supplies to feed the settlers, Sir Thomas Gates set out for England with Captain Newport, to bring the story of their miraculous survival to England, and English printers.

It came to the ears of Emanuel van Meteren by we know not what route. Like his earlier accounts of Virginia, this one is sufficiently accurate to indicate a source within the Virginia Company, and yet it has variations, interpretations, and some inaccuracies which prove that it is no slavish copy of any known narrative of the Bermuda adventure.

His error in stating that Captain Newport, who brought Gates back to England, had taken Lord Delaware out to Virginia can be overlooked as a bit of confusion in the mind of a man who had lived three quarters of a century and had just over a year left to live when he heard the Bermuda story. His statement of Gates's motives for returning are much more interesting to consider. The traditional version is that he was ordered back by the Virginia Company to report to them on the condition of the colony that he had almost abandoned. Van Meteren has him coming back to look into the rumor brought to Virginia that his command in Zeeland had been canceled as a result of the general belief that the *Sea Venture* and its passengers had perished at sea. Van Meteren's view is not an improbable one, for the leave that the States-General had granted to Gates in 1608 had been for one year only, and in December 1609, there was already concern in high circles that he might lose his company in the Netherlands, for Salisbury requested Sir Ralph Winwood to look into the rumor that certain English companies were about to be dismissed from service in the Netherlands and "it is feared he may be included in that generality, if some course be not taken to prevent it in the mean time." [23] Now again the English used Dutch interest in their Virginia en-

70]

terprise to secure a favor, as Salisbury asked Winwood to remind the States-General that Gates "is not returned from their service for any private occasions of his own, but for an enterprise of plantation in the Indies, where I am persuaded they would be glad the King of England and other Christian Princes might have a settling as well as the King of Spain." [24]

When Gates returned to England in September 1610, action was taken to make certain that his company in the Netherlands would be a dependable sinecure for him to return to after an even longer absence. Now he even had the king concerned to protect his interests, for in a letter of January 17, 1611, Salisbury wrote to Winwood again, stating, "Because it is conceived that the whole frame of the Plantation doth especially depend upon his personal assistance . . . his Majesty, favoring the good success thereof . . . hath commanded me to signify unto you that in his name you should deal effectively with the States to grant him leave to be absent three years, and not hazard the loss of his company." [25] Gates himself went to The Hague sometime after December 15, 1610, to present his case for retaining his company and for other discussions with the States-General. In a postscript to his letter Salisbury urged Winwood to send Gates back as soon as possible since he was to sail to Virginia shortly. [26] While Van Meteren does state that his story of the Bermuda adventure is based on that told by Gates, it does not follow that he had it directly from Gates. Still, his evaluation of Gates's concern for his company suggests a rather close knowledge of the captain's affairs.

Van Meteren's account of the landing on Bermuda and the life of the survivors there does not vary in the important points from other contemporary accounts. His figure of "at least 120" people on the *Sea Venture* at the time they arrived at Bermuda may be a typographical error for 150, the figure generally given. [27] Van Meteren's version is somewhat more rich in details of the primitive economy of the survivors in his mention of their housebuilding, distilling of salt water, and salvaging of iron from ships wrecked on Bermuda's shores. He does not describe the products of the island in as great detail as Jourdain, however.

The details of life on Bermuda probably interested the old historian less than the possibility of an English colony being established there. In this instance, as in earlier ones, he was quick to report plans under way in England for enterprises in America. His statement that a company was formed in 1611 indicates that he was recording events that year or early in 1612, well ahead of the third Virginia charter which provided for the settlement of Bermuda by a separate group of men within the Virginia Company. This charter was not in effect until June 1612, some two months after Van Meteren's death.[28] His statement on the company's intentions came true when, in early May, before the charter was finally approved, a group of sixty colonists set out in the *Plough* with Bermuda as their objective. Arriving on July 11, they found the three men who stayed on the island when the settlers from the *Sea Venture* departed for Virginia, and they asked these "natives" at once about the prospects for ambergris, pearls, and treasure.[29] Van Meteren's "four pieces of artillery" as the island's defense materialized in the form of four major defense positions, which included in their ordnance two guns from the wreck of the *Sea Venture*.[30]

The suggestion that Van Meteren makes regarding the probability of finding gold on the island is novel, for none of the other early descriptions of Bermuda mention gold as a possible product. Also, its alleged discovery by Dutch sailors raises the interesting implication that Dutch sailors had been there before the first English landing. Since their story came to Van Meteren's ears, they must have been taken off the island by another ship returning to England or Europe.

This story of the Dutch castaways appears to be an otherwise untold tale in the history of Bermuda, a history that is extremely spare from the time Peter Martyr charted the island in 1511 [31] to the landing of the Virginia group ninety-eight years later. Although it was known earlier, there is no record of any near approach to Bermuda before that of Juan Bermudez in 1515, which was described by his distinguished passenger, the historian Gonzalo Fernández de Oviedo y Valdés. The storms that frequently beset ships in that area quickly gave the place a bad name, and it

72]

may not have been until 1563 that another Spanish ship willfully called there. That occasion was only a quick visit by Don Pedro Mendenez de Avila, who was searching for his son and who at the same time was on his way to Florida to root out a French Huguenot settlement there.[32] Another Spaniard, Pedro de Aspide, knew enough about Bermuda to request pearl-fishing rights there in 1587, but nothing is known to have come of the request. Diego Ramirez was driven ashore there in 1603, and he wrote a lengthy description of the wild life he found. The only recorded English experience on Bermuda in the sixteenth century is that of Henry May; he was picked up in the West Indies by a group of Frenchmen in 1593, and they ran aground at Bermuda, more as a result of wine-troubled minds than of the storms that usually were the cause of such havoc.

It is, of course, entirely possible that Van Meteren's narrative of the Dutch sailors landing on Bermuda is true, for the detailed account of their finding of gold suggests an actual experience. The particles in the water which they identified as gold were probably sediment of another kind, for there appears to have been no serious effort among the Bermuda adventurers to "investigate further."

The frankness with which Van Meteren had criticized the government of Virginia earlier is again apparent in his statement that the great disorder in which Gates and Somers found the Virginia colony was due to bad government. He is referring to the governorship of George Percy, who had been placed in charge of the colony in September 1609. This may have been an unduly harsh evaluation of a government which was struggling with problems perhaps beyond its power to solve with the authority and resources given it. Certainly Gates did not feel competent to revitalize the colony, and was quick enough to give it up and prepare to return the settlers to England. Nevertheless, it is apparent from Van Meteren's description of Virginia as a country rich in all sorts of natural products "so that they were well provided for" that the fault lay primarily with men rather than nature.

It was probably the failure of the colony's governors to exercise disciplinary power that evoked Van Meteren's criticism, for this was of deep concern to the Virginia Company itself. The mood of William Crashaw's sermon was upon the company, and upon Lord Delaware when he took the reins of government on Virginia's soil in June 1610. He let it be known that he believed the difficulties of the colony were due in no small part to the idleness and vanity of the settlers, and that he intended to bring an end to such attitudes even if this necessitated drawing "the sworde of justice." [33] He assured his superiors in London that things would improve, and he echoed Crashaw as he promised "he that knew not the way of goodness before, but cherished singularitie and faction, now can beate but a path himself of industrie and goodnes for others to trade in, such, may I well say, is the power of exemplar vertue." [34]

There was a brief restoration of morale under the administration of Lord Delaware, yet troubles persisted, for Virginia's ailments were not merely the lack of discipline and ambition among its inhabitants. There was the physical problem of adjusting to a new environment, and of survival in the face of diseases that swept through the colony. Many of those who lived through the Bermuda episode succumbed to the first shock of the "sickly season" in Virginia which carried off some one hundred fifty colonists during the summer of 1610. While Gates was in England looking to the maintenance of his command in Zeeland, Lord Delaware too fell ill, first with "a hot and violent Ague which held me a time," then "I began to be distempered with other greevous sickness, which successively & severally assailed me: for besides a relapse into the former disease . . . the Flux surprised me and kept me many daies, & afterward the Gout afflicted me in such sort, that making my body through weaknesse unable to stirre . . . drew upon me the disease called Scurvy . . . till I was upon the point to leave the world." [35]

Lord Delaware survived this siege of illness, but he was lost to Virginia, for he was forced to return to England to recover his health. As a collector of pamphlets, Emanuel van Meteren might well have picked up a copy of the governor's *Relation* which was published in 1611 to silence those who whispered about London that he had returned because of the poverty of the colony as others had done, or wanted to do. He insisted, however, that the succession of illnesses that had plagued him alone had driven him out of the colony, and that it was a place of great promise. He reported favorably on the soil of Virginia, the trade with the Indians, the state of the livestock, and other things likely to interest the backers of the enterprise.

While disease in Virginia steadily reduced its inhabitants, the Spanish ambassador in London, Don Alonso de Velasco, continued to give thought to the quickest means of removing the survivors from the miseries of the New World, and of preventing any further colonization there by the English. On September 30, 1610, he noted plans to send three additional ships with men, women, preachers, and armaments to Virginia in the following January, and he recommended that this might best be forestalled if the king of Spain would just send out a few ships to drive the remaining colonists from their settlement.[36]

The three ships Don Alonso had in mind apparently were those being readied by the Virginia Company to take Captain Thomas Dale and a group of colonists and livestock out to Virginia. Dale bore the title of "High Marshall" and went prepared to establish "laws, divine, morall and martiall,"[37] a severe code that became even more so in the hands of a severe man, a soldier of long experience in the Netherlands, for Dale had been in service there as early as 1588. Like Gates, Dale was granted a leave of absence by the Dutch, but his leave was to extend for three years; despite Winwood's petition to the States-General, however, Dale's pay was to be discontinued during his absence.[38]

Arriving in Virginia in May, Dale set to work to put the colony in order, and he is to be credited with improvements which assured its continuance. These improvements were partly in the realm of law, but it was probably in public health that he made his most significant contribution, for he moved the major settlement about fifty miles up the river to a place called Dutch Gap, the new settlement being named Henrico.[39] This place was less subject to disease than the lower and less arable area around Jamestown. Improvement also in the domestic economy of the settlers seems to have followed Dale's order that each family was to have three acres to raise crops for household use, thus breaching the system of community-held land which had prevailed since the beginning of the colony.

The hand that gave health and food, however, carried a whip, and at times a sword, for Captain Dale regarded discipline as of equal importance to the survival of the colony. When some of the settlers refused to apply themselves to the building of the new community, he ordered eight of the insubordinates put to death.[40] In his attitude toward discipline, Dale reflected the views of the Virginia Company.

Dale's major administrative experience had been military, but his judgments on non-military matters were also excellent in some cases. Samuel Purchas hailed him as "the best establisher of the Virginia Plantation." [41] Purchas, however, was never in Virginia, and many of those who were regarded Dale as a cruel tyrant. Whether or not cruelty was a basic trait of his character, ingrained through years of service in the Netherlands, Dale could find justification for his actions in the laws he was required to enforce. Charity and forgiveness were no part of the English Puritan spirit as it expressed itself in the "laws, divine, morall and martiall." The law was made known along with the punishment for transgression of it. Reasons for disobedience were little considered. Impious speech against the Trinity or the Articles of Religion was punishable by death, and blasphemy likewise, on the third offense. Disrespect toward ministers of religion called for whipping; absence from worship brought loss of provisions for the first offense, whipping for the second, and six months in the galleys for the third. Independent trading with the Indians was a capital offense, as was any form of misappropriation of the company's supplies.

Under such a code, and an army man to execute it, the discipline in Virginia became so harsh that men who had feared the savages of the hinterland now fled to them when they ran afoul of colony law. Here again we find a meeting of the English and Dutch ways of life, for these onerous laws were for the most part the work of Gates and Dale, neither of them lawyers, but men whose attitudes toward discipline had been shaped by military experience in the Netherlands; the nature of the grim conflict there tended to stress the result desired, with little regard for human frailties.[42] In Virginia too the responsibility of Gates and Dale was to assure a result: the survival of the colony. This they accomplished.

More than good health, limited prosperity, and severe discipline, however, seemed needed in 1611 to guarantee the continuance of Virginia. The Spanish ambassador in London was urging the destruction of the colony, and other diplomats heard rumblings of Spanish preparations for an attack on Virginia. The Dutch seemed to feel that England might now need the old alliance again. Late in 1610, or early the next year, when Sir Thomas Gates went to The Hague to confer about his commission, he also planned to discuss Anglo-Dutch cooperation in Virginia, for Sir Noel Caron, the Dutch ambassador in London, had made a proposal for "joining with us in that Collonie." [43] This would not have been an unlikely course at that time, for in Guiana, where Spain kept a very close watch on interlopers, the Dutch and English continued to cooperate,[44] and in the East Indies there was still harmony to the end of 1610. That the Dutch were more willing to become partners than the English were to have them may be indicated in John More's comment to Sir Ralph Winwood on the Dutch proposal for alliance in the East Indies. "We fear," he said, "that in case of joyning, if it be upon equal Terms, the Art and Industry of the people will wear out ours." [45] Considering the comments made on the industry of the earliest settlers of Virginia by Van Meteren, Captain John Smith, and others, it might have been just such a fear that kept Virginia from becoming an Anglo-Dutch colony at this time.

If the old legend of Dutch superiority and niggardliness prevented a commercial alliance between the two peoples, the need of each for military and naval assistance to meet the threat from Spain kept the alliance very much on the minds of diplomats in the last year of Van Meteren's life. There was greater confidence in peace at James's court than there was at the English embassy in Madrid, despite the fact that Don Alonso de Velasco from London continued to urge his king to wipe out the Virginia colony. From Madrid Ambassador Francis Cottington wrote, "I have some cause to fear that certaine Gallions built now at Havanna are meant for Virginia, there to do some Mischief to our Plantations." [46] To meet such an emergency Captain Dale was asking for 2000 men in Virginia, and when in the summer of 1611 three Spaniards came ashore in Virginia they were made prisoners, which brought a stiff letter of protest from the king of Spain to James I.[47] But James kept a cool head, and while London was filled with rumors of Spanish designs on Ireland and Virginia, John More seems to have reflected the royal attitude when he advised Winwood that the government did not worry about such reports, "Neither is it likely indeed that the King of Spaine will break so profitable a Peace." [48]

It is very probable, however, that had the Virginia enterprise involved any sort of naval-military conflict, England would gladly have accepted Dutch assistance, for when their own weakness in an area became apparent, the English were eager enough for the closest possible relations with the Dutch. In the East Indies, for example, where the threat to English trade was the Dutch themselves, Ambassador Winwood was anxious for them to "take hold of the offer which is tendered to joyne in consort with this people in their trade to those parts, and both nations make and be, but one company . . . and be master over the Portugal in those islands." [49]

Dutch reasons for wanting a partnership in America are easily understood. This was Spain's stronghold, despite her gradual decline; as Virginia was proving, settlement would be a slow process and success could only be assured by a strong fleet or a charitable Spanish monarch. If the Dutch were to have any interest in the New World, they must ultimately fight the Spaniards to establish it. A base within the boundaries of Virginia would be most valuable in carrying on such a fight.

The extent of Dutch knowledge about and interest in North America was probably greater than is positively recorded. Dutch merchants, for instance, appear to have followed up Hudson's voyage of 1610. Joannes

De Laet states that Dutch merchants sent a ship to the Hudson River later that year,[50] and Nicolaes à Wassenaer tells of a voyage by Hendrick Christianszoon of Cleves who apparently came up that way from a voyage to the southern part of North America or the Caribbean, but did not stop at "the River Montagne, called Mauritius by us,"[51] because his ship was laden and because a ship from Monickendam had previously been wrecked in that area. The date of the voyage is not recorded by Wassenaer, but probably it was not later than 1611, and if a ship of Monickendam had already been wrecked there between Hudson's voyage and that of Christianszoon, there must have been a quick follow-up of the former.

The coast of North America was sufficiently interesting to Captain Jan Corneliszoon May to bring him there in the winter of 1611–12.[52] He sailed northeastward in search of a passage to the Pacific, as Hudson had done, in the summer of 1611. When winter came upon him in those northerly latitudes above Norway, he turned westward, and by October 24 was off the coast of Newfoundland. He proceeded southwestwardly, giving Dutch place-names to points along the way until he arrived at Cape Cod Bay. When spring appeared to be on its way, Captain May returned to his search for the northeast passage.

In 1611 also an enterprise in the Hudson River with definite commercial objectives was undertaken. A ship, the *St. Pieter*, was chartered by three Dutch merchants on May 19. The captain, Cornelis Rijser of Amsterdam, sailed with a crew of thirteen and in addition took three supercargoes for the merchants. The destination given was "Terra Nova," and a load of goods was taken for trade with the Indians.[53] It appears that the voyage was a success, for the same merchants were involved in voyages to the Hudson River in 1612 and 1613, and they were among the founders of the first trading company established for the express purpose of developing the Hudson River trade. From these early Dutch voyages to the northern part of Virginia, successors to Henry Hudson's expedition, came the New Netherland colony which established Dutch laws, customs, religion, and business enterprise for more than half a century.[54]

Emanuel van Meteren lived until April 8, 1612, and apparently his interest in the events of his time continued until very near the end of his life, for the last event he recorded was the death of the archbishop of Bavaria on February 17 of that year. Considering the time it must have taken the news to reach London, it is unlikely that it would have come to his attention much more than a month before his death. As if his restless mind sensed that the end was near, Van Meteren wrote frequently of death in the last months, most of his *History* for late 1611 and early 1612 being little but a catalog of obituaries of prominent persons who had died.

In the summer of 1611 he did add one last note on Virginia, an entry of little consequence, but evidence that it was on his mind, just as America was on the minds of other Dutchmen that year. He wrote: "They have made preparations in England to send more ships and people to Virginia where farther inland they have built brick fortresses and city walls, as well as houses, and have planted vineyards, hops, and other necessities." [55] This final observation on Virginia is on the second to last folio of the book, and is placed between two items dated August 1611. It is followed by a brief note on plans to send ships to the northwest passage that Henry Hudson was believed to have found. This was the voyage of Thomas Button, which set out with great optimism in 1612.

Brick fortresses, houses, vineyards, all imply permanence and an end to the idleness, factionalism, and misgovernment that had characterized Virginia, and that Van Meteren had reported with frankness. By August 1611, when these words were written, Gates had returned to Virginia, taking with him more settlers and livestock. There were seven hundred people in the colony now, and if they were not happy under the rule of Gates and Dale, they were healthier than they had been, and busier. The Virginia colony was taking on an air of stability, perhaps even in the mind of Emanuel van Meteren.

There were still disquieting signs. Even as Van Meteren made his optimistic note in London, Captain Dale was writing from Virginia requesting more and better men, both for work and for meeting the constant Indian menace. He also wrote of the three Spaniards he had taken prisoner, defending his action by saying that he had prevented these sailors from spreading their knowledge of the location of the settlements and their weak, unfortified condition.[56] Also that August in London, in response to a message from Philip III, the Spanish ambassador assured his monarch that he would see to it that dependable spies were placed aboard the next ship for Virginia so that Spain might be kept informed of the Virginia and Bermuda developments.[57] On February 25, 1612, Philip again ordered his emissary to send spies aboard ships for Virginia to ascertain "the nature of the enterprise." [58] Nor was all the tension of that time concealed in diplomatic correspondence. That same month Spanish garrisons in the southern Netherlands were to be reinforced with 1500 men, and before they sailed there was concern in the English embassy in Madrid that some ships of the fleet assembled to carry these troops were bound for Virginia.[59] In an even more alarmed state of mind, the English ambassador in the Spanish capital, Sir John Digby, reported on March 9 that it was his understanding that Spain would run any risk rather than let the Virginia colony survive.[60]

It may have appeared to many Englishmen that the old enemy was about to show his true colors again, and that the defenders of the reformed faith must stand together once more in the Low Countries, in the Channel, and in the West Indies. But these were men with their minds on the past. True, Spain could threaten, and could destroy Virginia if she chose to accept the consequences. But a generation had passed since Spain's finest hour. The future in the East and West Indies belonged to England and France and the Netherlands, and the time was close at hand when the English and Dutch must determine between themselves to whom the longer future really belonged. Even as Sir John Digby recorded his worries and conjectures about Spain in Madrid, Englishmen in the East Indies wrote that they were being deprived of the freedom to trade in certain islands where they felt they had rights, and that the enemy here was the Dutch merchant.[61]

London and The Hague tackled the problem of insuring orderly conduct of the East Indian trade between rival merchants far from the restraining hands of government. Salisbury urged Winwood to present the English merchants' complaint, and to secure restraint on the part of the Dutch "until such time as some means may be thought of to prevent these differences." [62] Winwood went to the States-General and based his case on the right of the freedom of commerce, an argument which was ultimately to engage the talents of Hugo Grotius. Yet when Winwood's argument was made, and when he had satisfied himself that the States-General wanted nothing but peace with England, he saw no means to achieve continued harmony in the East Indies, for he warned that the Dutch East India Company was "influentiall, powerful and mighty in this State, and will not acknowledge the authority of the States generall, more than shalbe for their private profit." [63]

Winwood's observation could have been easily applied to merchants and sea captains of several countries at that time, and the English merchant who wished for Dutch help in the West Indies could shortly be fighting Dutchmen in the East Indies, merely by leaving the New World for trade in the East.[64] Such was the state of international and mercantile anarchy when Emanuel van Meteren died, and the alliance so natural in his lifetime gave way to the logical outcome of unrestrained commercial rivalry. Englishmen and Dutchmen were shortly to seek each other out in the East Indies, in Africa, in America, and to kill, burn, plunder, and destroy with a hate their fathers and grandfathers had reserved only for Spaniards. And so their long friendship was interrupted as they adhered to the rule of international politics which says there are no continuous friends, no continuous enemies, only policy is continuous.

Notes and Index

NOTES

THE ANGLO-DUTCH ALLIANCE

[1] John Adams, *A Memorial to Their High Mightinesses, the States General of the United Provinces of the Low Countries* (n.p., n.d.). The memorial was delivered on April 19, 1781, and was probably published shortly thereafter.

[2] For a presentation of Dutch influence on England and America by an ardent partisan, see Douglas Campbell, *The Puritan in Holland, England and America* (2 vols.; New York, 1893).

It is necessary to make clear what I mean by the term "Dutch" in this book, for modern usage based upon the subsequent political division of the Low Countries does not apply to political and cultural divisions of the sixteenth and seventeenth centuries. By "Dutch" is meant the peoples and territory of the Dutch-speaking northern portion of the Low Countries, comprising about four-fifths of their total area. The term "Fleming" was frequently used in the sixteenth and seventeenth centuries for the people of Flanders, the southeastern portion of the Dutch-speaking area. The term "Dutch" may be used for this region as well, but a resident of the county of Flanders may also be referred to as a Fleming. In using the term "Netherlands," I refer to the entire seventeen provinces under the control of Philip II at his accession, and "the Low Countries" has a like meaning. See P. Geyl's preface to his *The Revolt of the Netherlands* (London, 1932) for a brief discussion and maps relating to modern and earlier usage of these terms.

[3] F. J. Fisher, "Commercial Trends and Policy in Sixteenth Century England," *Economic History Review*, 10:97 (November 1940).

[4] Sir George Warner, ed., *The Libelle of Englyshe Polycye* (Oxford, 1926), p. 5.

[5] *Ibid.*, pp. 5–6.

[6] Ephraim Lipson, *The History of the Woolen and Worsted Industries* (London, 1921), pp. 12–13.

[7] Ephraim Lipson, *A Short History of Wool and Its Manufacture* (London, 1953), p. 50.

[8] Thomas Fuller, *The Church History of Britain* (3 vols.; London, 1842), I, 419.

[9] W. J. B. Pienaar, *English Influences in Dutch Literature and Justus Van Effen as Intermediary* (Cambridge, England, 1929), p. 2.

[85

[10] T. de Vries, *Holland's Influence on English Language and Literature* (Chicago, 1916), pp. 145–148; J. F. Bense, *A Dictionary of the Low-Dutch Element in English Vocabulary* (The Hague, 1939). This latter work contains 5079 English words with indication of their relationship to Dutch usage. See also G. N. Clark, *The Dutch Influence on the English Vocabulary*, Society for Pure English, Tract No. XLIV (Oxford, 1939); J. F. Bense, *Anglo-Dutch Relations from the Earliest Times to the Death of William the Third* (The Hague, 1925), pp. 3–4.

[11] Bense, *Anglo-Dutch Relations*, p. 4.

[12] Henry R. Plomer, "The Importation of Low Country and French Books into England, 1480 and 1502–3," *Library*, 4th series, 9:164 (September 1928).

[13] J. F. Mozley, *Coverdale and His Bibles* (London, 1953), pp. 72–74. Jacob van Meteren was the publisher of the Coverdale Bible, but the printer and place of printing have been subjects of much dispute. Mozley (see pp. 74–77) supports the theory that it was printed in Cologne by either Cervicorn or Soter, printers who are known to have produced Lutheran books previously.

[14] Bense, *Anglo-Dutch Relations*, p. 97.

[15] John S. Burn, *The History of the French, Walloon, Dutch and Other Foreign Protestant Refugees Settled in England* (London, 1846), pp. 186–190; John Strype, *Annals of the Reformation and Establishment of Religion . . . during the First Twelve Years of Queen Elizabeth's Happy Reign* (London, 1709), p. 386.

[16] W. D. Verduyn, *Emanuel van Meteren* (The Hague, 1926), pp. 37–72. No satisfactory biography of Van Meteren has yet been written. Details of his birth, marriages, business connections, and death were included in the 1614 edition of his *History* in a brief statement by Simon Ruytinck. Verduyn has expanded this, but the absence of any considerable manuscript material in Van Meteren's hand has been a major obstacle to the writing of an adequate biography.

[17] Johannes Radermacher to Jacob Cool, Middelburg, 25 July 1603, in J. H. Hessels, *Ecclesiae Londino-Batavae Archivum* (2 vols.; Cambridge, England, 1887–97), I, 772–779 (hereafter cited as Hessels).

[18] Jacob Cool to Abraham Ortelius, London, 25 January 1591, in Hessels, I, 458–462.

[19] R. E. G. and E. F. Kirk, eds., "Returns of Aliens Dwelling in the City and Suburbs of London from the Reign of Henry VIII to That of James I," *Publications of the Huguenot Society of London*, Vol. X, Part 2 (1902), pp. 203–212.

[20] A. F. Scott Pearson, *Thomas Cartwright and Elizabethan Puritanism* (Cambridge, England, 1925), pp. 175–185.

[21] Burn, *History of . . . Refugees*, pp. 3–4.

[22] John Strype, *The History of the Life and Acts of . . . Edmund Grindal* (London, 1720), pp. 42, 44, 51.

[23] Sir John Hawkins, *A True Declaration of the Troublesome Voyadge . . . to the Partes of Guynea and the West Indies* (London, 1596).

[24] John Lothrop Motley, *History of the United Netherlands* (4 vols.; New York, 1870–74), pp. 285–326.

[25] Richard Hakluyt, *The Principal Navigations, Voiages Traffiques and Discoveries of the English Nation* (3 vols.; London, 1598–99) I, 591; translated from Van Meteren's *History*, probably from the 1596 or 1597 edition.

[26] *Ibid.*

[27] *Ibid.*, p. 600.

[28] *Ibid.*, p. 609.

[29] John Stow, *Annals*, quoted in Bense, *Anglo-Dutch Relations*, p. 162.

[30] William B. Rye, *England as Seen by Foreigners in the Days of Elizabeth and James I* (London, 1865), p. 70.

[31] Eden's translation of Martin Cortes's *Arte de navegar* in 1568 gave to English pilots their best book up to that time on the techniques of navigation. He also published *A Treatise of the New India*, 1553, and *The Decades of the Newe Worlde*, 1555, with an enlarged edition appearing in 1577. John Frampton made five translations from the Spanish: Nicholas Monarde's *Joyful Newes out of the Newe Found Worlde*, 1577; Martin Fernandez de Enciso's *A Brief Description of the Portes, Creekes, Bayes, and Havens of the Weast India*, 1578; Bernardino de Escalante's *A Discourse of the Navigation which the Portugales Doe Make . . .* 1579; Marco Polo's *The Most Famous Travels of Marcus Paulus*, 1579; and Francisco de Thamara's *A Discoverie of the Countries of Tartaria, Scithia and Cataya*, 1580.

[32] *Die Nieuwe Weerelt* (Antwerp, 1563). This collection of travels was compiled by J. Huttich and edited by Simon Grynaeus. The translation into Dutch was made from the German by Cornelis Ablyn.

[33] *Descriptionis Ptolemaicae augmentum* (Louvain, 1597).

[34] *Itinerario, Voyage ofte Schipvaert . . . naer Oost ofte Portugaels Indien* (Amsterdam, 1596). The English edition appeared in 1598, and a Latin edition the following year. The first French edition was published in 1610.

[35] The first attempt was made under the command of George Raymond and James Lancaster. The storm destroyed one ship, and the other ended up in the West Indies, whence Lancaster and a few hands returned home in a French ship. The second voyage, commanded by Benjamin Wood, was a failure also, with only one survivor returning to England.

[36] Sir William Foster, *England's Quest for Eastern Trade* (London, 1933), pp. 147–155.

[37] J. Franklin Jameson, "Willem Usselinx, Founder of the Dutch and Swedish West India Companies," *Papers of the American Historical Association*, Vol. II, No. 3 (1887), pp. 1–31.

[38] Two other Dutch histories that were inspired by the war of liberation were Pieter Christiansz. Bor's *Begin ende Vervolg der Nederlandsche Oorlogen*, published between 1595 and 1602, and Everhard Van Reyd's *Historie der Nederlant-*

scher Oorlogen, which carried the narrative of the war to 1601 but was not published until 1626.

[39] Hogenberg was the engraver of many of the maps in the *Theatrum Orbis Terrarum* of Abraham Ortelius. The first edition of the Hogenberg plates with Van Meteren's text was probably printed by Nicholaus Henricus of Ober Ursel, a town in Nassau. See Verduyn, *Emanuel van Meteren*, pp. 156–167. The title of this edition was *Historia unnd Abcontrafeytungh, furnemlich der Niderlandischer Geschichten, und Kriegszhendelen.*

[40] Van Meteren supplied the additional text for these enlargements. The Hogenberg illustrations were omitted and portraits substituted. The one-volume edition of 1596 was titled *Historia oder Eigentliche und warhaffte Beschreibung aller Kriegshandel unnd gedenkwurdigen Geschichten . . .* Some copies of the 1597 reprint have the imprint Hamburg, François van Dort, 1596, which appears to be a deception. Verduyn believes that all these reprints may have been the work of Arnold Mylius of Cologne. See *Emanuel van Meteren*, p. 174. The Latin edition was probably also published by Mylius, under the title *Historia Belgica . . .*

[41] Verduyn, *Emanuel van Meteren*, pp. 179–203. The Dutch edition of 1599 was titled *Belgische ofte Nederlantsche Historie, van onsen Tijden.* It is unlikely that the States-General was able to enforce its prohibition upon the sale of the book in the Netherlands. It must in fact have been popular there, for Vennecool planned another edition in Dutch. The States-General specified that corrections must be made by the author, but Vennecool ignored this requirement and published a new edition in 1605. Van Meteren refused to accept this edition as authentic. This 1605 edition does not add any material after 1598, and it has the same title as the 1599 edition. There is, however, in the British Museum a German edition published by Johan Jansen, *Historia, oder eigentlische und warhaffte Beschreibung aller furnehmen Kriegshandel . . .* (Arnhem, 1604), which includes twenty books, one more than the 1599 Dutch edition, and brings the narrative up through 1604. A second title page introduces the material from 1599 to 1604.

[42] Van Meteren, 1598 Latin ed., p. 436.

[43] George Bruner Parks, *Richard Hakluyt and the English Voyages* (New York, 1928), pp. 143–145, 253. Van Meteren's letters to the treasurer of Zeeland are published in S. P. L'Honoré Naber, ed., *Reizen van Willem Barents, Jacob van Heemskerck, Jan Cornelisz Rijp en Anderen naar het Noorden* (The Hague, 1917), pp. 201–210. Hakluyt's letter to Van Meteren stating the conditions under which he would do the work, and Van Meteren's letter to the treasurer of Zeeland in which he recommends Hakluyt, are published in E. G. R. Taylor, ed., *The Original Writings and Correspondence of the Two Richard Hakluyts* (2 vols.; London, 1935), II, 417–419.

BEGINNINGS IN VIRGINIA

[1] Hessels, II, 922–923.

[2] David Harris Willson, *James VI and I* (London, 1956), p. 207.

[3] *Ibid.*

[4] Historical Manuscripts Commission, *Report on the Manuscripts of the Duke of Buccleuch and Queensberry, Preserved at Montague House, Whitehall* (3 vols.; London, 1899), I, 58.

[5] Earl of Salisbury to Ralph Winwood, 7 June 1606, in *Memorials of Affairs of State in the Reigns of Queen Elizabeth and King James. Collected Chiefly from the Original Papers of Sir Ralph Winwood* (3 vols.; London, 1725), II, 219 (hereafter cited as *Winwood Memorials*).

[6] Salisbury to Winwood, 7 June 1606, in *Winwood Memorials*, II, 217–219.

[7] Sir Dudley Carleton, a member of England's diplomatic corps, showed concern for the possibility of a reduction of English forces in the Low Countries after the conclusion of peace in his letter to John Chamberlain, 25 December 1606 (*State Papers, Domestic,* Public Record Office, 14/24:29). Chamberlain is remembered primarily as a writer of letters to England's prominent figures. See Wallace Notestein's biographical essay, "John Chamberlain," in *Four Worthies* (New Haven, 1957), pp. 29–119.

[8] Ferdinando Gorges to Salisbury, 20 March 1607, in *Cecil Papers*, vol. 120, fol. 130. (Microfilm of the originals at Hatfield House were consulted at the British Museum, Department of Manuscripts.)

[9] Gorges to Privy Council, 1 October 1607, in *Cecil Papers*, vol. 122, fol. 107.

[10] Edmund Scott, *An Exact Discourse of the Subtilties, Fashisions, Pollicies, Religion, and Ceremonies of the East Indians* (London, 1606), fol. C2 verso. Scott was the first English factor at Bantam, and his book contains numerous instances of relations, both friendly and competitive, between the English and Dutch there.

[11] Two small books published in England describing Portuguese defeats in the East Indies are *A True and Perfect Relation of the Newes Sent from Amsterdam, the 21 of February, 1603* (London, 1603) and Cornelis Matelief, *An Historical and True Discourse of a Voyage Made into the East Indies* (London, 1608).

[12] Jameson, "Willem Usselinx," pp. 30–34.

[13] Salisbury to Winwood, 2 April 1607, 20 April 1607, 8 May 1607, in *Winwood Memorials*, pp. 298–299, 305–306, 309–310.

[14] George Edmundson, *Anglo-Dutch Rivalry during the First Half of the Seventeenth Century* (Oxford, 1911) p. 17; Willson, *James VI and I*, p. 278.

[15] Instructions from His Majesty to Sir Richard Spencer and Sir Ralph Winwood, in *State Papers, Holland*, 84/66:52.

[16] *Ibid.*, 84/66:63.

[17] *Ibid.*, 84/66:59.

[18] Charles Cornwallis to Sir Thomas Edmondes, 15 October 1608, in *Stowe Mss.* (British Museum, Department of Manuscripts), 170, fol. 210. Cornwallis was the ambassador to Spain from 1605 to 1609. Edmondes was at this time the English ambassador in Brussels.

[19] Cornwallis to Edmondes, 3 July 1608, in *Stowe Mss.* 170, fol. 79.

[20] David B. Quinn, *Raleigh and the British Empire* (London, 1947), p. 215.

[21] Alexander Brown, *The Genesis of the United States* (2 vols.; Boston and New York, 1891), I, 25.

[22] *Ibid.*, I, 45–46.

[23] *Ibid.*, I, 46.

[24] The title of the 1608 edition was *Commentarien ofte Memorien van-den Nedderlandtschen Staet, Handel, Oorloghen ende Gheschiedenissen van onsen Tyden, etc.* Despite the publisher's attempt to conceal his location behind the imprint "Schotlandt buyten Danswijck by Hermes van Loven" it is quite certain that this edition was printed in Amsterdam. It extends through 1607 in twenty-eight books. An appendix was added and is usually found in the volume. It consists of twenty-seven folios and bears the imprint "Tot London voor Emanuel van Meteren, 1609."

[25] Brown, *Genesis*, I; Samuel Purchas, *Purchas His Pilgrimes* (5 vols.; London, 1625), IV, 1683.

[26] Robert A. Brock, "Virginia, 1606–1689," in Justin Winsor, ed., *Narrative and Critical History of America* (8 vols.; Boston, 1885), III, 153.

[27] William Stith, *The History of the First Discovery and Settlement of Virginia* (New York, 1865), p. 46. This is a reprint of the first edition of 1747.

[28] *State Papers, Domestic*, 14/28:34.

[29] John Pory was a close friend of Richard Hakluyt, and in 1600 translated the description of Africa by Leo Africanus at Hakluyt's request. He became a member of Parliament in 1605, and subsequently traveled in France, the Low Countries, Ireland, and Turkey. He was in Virginia in 1619 and 1623 as secretary to Governor Yeardley. The Mr. Warner mentioned in the letter may have been the poet and attorney William Warner who was patronized by Henry and Sir George Carey, or possibly Thomas Warner who ultimately became the founder of an English settlement on St. Christopher's Island, the first English settlement in the islands of the West Indies.

[30] Thomas Smith to Salisbury, 17 August 1607, in *Cecil Papers*, vol. 122, fol. 23.

[31] See Brock, "Virginia, 1606–1689," p. 129.

[32] Stith, *History of the First Discovery*, p. 47.

[33] Brock, "Virginia, 1606–1689," p. 131, places the total number of this "first supply" at 120 and states that Captain Nelson brought seventy settlers in the *Phoenix*. The earliest account of the arrival of these two ships is contained in Captain John Smith's *A True Relation of Such Occurrences and Accidents of Noate as Hath Hapned in Virginia* (London, 1608). It does not, however, record the number of men brought by Newport and Nelson.

[34] See below, p. 36.

[35] Brown, *Genesis*, I, 89.

[36] *Ibid.*

[37] *Ibid.*, 91.

[38] *Ibid.*, 119.

[39] *Ibid.*, 120–122.

[40] Salisbury to Cornwallis, 18 November 1607, in *Winwood Memorials*, II, 357–359.

[41] *Ibid.*

[42] Jameson, "Willem Usselinx," pp. 30–34.

[43] *State Papers, Holland*, 84/66(Pt. 1):81. The inscription on the cover reads *The Patent of the States General to the Merchants of the West Indies. Translated out of Dutch.*

[44] These pamphlets, generally considered to be thirty-eight in number, were issued separately; a collective preface was given to them by the bookseller and they were sold as a lot. Some of the pamphlets in "The Dutch Beehive" were written by Willem Usselinx (Jameson, pp. 35–45). For a list of the individual titles see G. M. Asher, *A Bibliographical and Historical Essay on the Dutch Books and Pamphlets Relating to New Netherland* (Amsterdam, 1854–67), pp. 86–89.

[45] Van Meteren, 1608 ed., Appendix, fol. 19 recto.

[46] Thomas J. Wertenbaker, *Virginia under the Stuarts, 1607–1688* (New York, 1959), pp. 4–5.

[47] Edward Arber, ed., *Travels and Works of Captain John Smith* (2 vols.; Edinburgh, 1910), I, lxxxv–lxxxvi.

[48] Captain Nelson returned to London about July 1, 1608, and his arrival was noted in a letter from John Chamberlain to Sir Dudley Carleton of that date. See Thomas Birch, ed., *The Court and Times of James the First* (2 vols.; London, 1848), I, 76.

[49] Cornwallis to the Privy Council, 19 April 1608, in *Winwood Memorials*, II, 386–388.

[50] Cornwallis to the Privy Council, 17 May 1608, in *Winwood Memorials*, II, 399–400.

[51] Cornwallis to Salisbury, 3 July 1608, in *State Papers, Spain*, 94/15:77.

[52] Sir John Ogle to Salisbury, 21 February 1608, *State Papers, Holland*, 84/66 (Pt. 1):97. Pt. 1, fol. 97. Ogle typified the Englishman devoted to the Dutch cause. He went to the Low Countries as a soldier in 1591, remained there in that capacity until the truce, and after that was named governor of Utrecht by the States-General. He was, nevertheless, interested in America, and became a member of the Virginia Company in 1609.

[53] Winwood to Şir Thomas Edmondes, 6 November 1608, in *Stowe Mss.*, 170, fol. 230.

[54] Sir Henry Neville to Winwood, 21 June 1608, in *Winwood Memorials*, II, 411–412. Neville was a member of Parliament from 1584 until his death in 1615. He served as ambassador to France in 1599 and 1600. He was inclined to Puritanism, and his views in Parliament were not those of his sovereign.

[55] John More to Winwood, 25 June 1608, in *Winwood Memorials*, II, 412–413. This is probably the John More who was recorder of Winchester and M.P. for Winchester in 1597 and from 1604 to 1611. He was a subscriber to the Virginia Company.

[56] Motley, *History of the United Netherlands*, IV, 465.

[57] Smith, *A True Relation*, fol. E4 verso. Smith's book was entered with the Company of Stationers on August 13, 1608, which was more than a month after Van Meteren composed his final note on Virginia for his 1608 edition.

DUTCH AND ENGLISH VOYAGES

[1] E. B. O'Callaghan, ed., *Documents Relative to the Colonial History of the State of New York* (15 vols.; Albany, 1853–87), I, 2.

[2] William Symonds, *Virginia. A Sermon Preached at White-Chappel, in the Presence of Many . . . Planters for Virginia* (London, 1609), p. 1.

[3] *Ibid.*, p. 9.

[4] *Ibid.*, pp. 13–14.

[5] *Ibid.*, pp. 53–54.

[6] Robert Johnson, *Nova Britannia. Offering Most Excellent Fruites by Planting in Virginia* (London, 1609).

[7] *Ibid.*, fol. C1 recto.

[8] Robert Gray, *A Good Speed to Virginia* (London, 1609), fol. A3 recto.

[9] Daniel Price, *Sauls Prohibition Staide . . . with a Reproofe of Those That Traduce the Honourable Plantation of Virginia* (London, 1609), fol. F3 recto.

[10] *Ibid.*, fols. F1 verso, F2 recto.

[11] Ferdinand de Soto, *Virginia Richly Valued*, Richard Hakluyt, trans. (London, 1609).

[12] Marc Lescarbot, *Nova Francia*, Pierre Erondelle, trans. (London, 1609). Two issues were published in 1609. This translation contained only portions of the original work by Lescarbot which was also published for the first time in 1609.

[13] Brown, *Genesis*, I, 244.

[14] *Ibid.*, pp. 244–246.

[15] Zuñiga to Philip III, 1 April 1609, in Brown, *Genesis*, I, 254–255.

[16] "Instructions given to Capt. Thomas Holcroft," 29 May 1609, in Brown, *Genesis*, I, 316–318.

[17] *Ibid.*

[18] See p. 18 above.

[19] Van Meteren, 1609 ed., fol. 162 recto. In the 1614 edition it was changed to Henri Hudson; see fol. 572. See also Henry C. Murphy, *Henry Hudson in Holland* (The Hague, 1909), p. 140.

[20] Following the 1608 edition with the 1609 appendix, another edition appeared with the appendix imprint "London voor Emanuel van Meteren, 1610." Superficially there appears to be no difference between these two editions apart from the inclusion of nine more folios in the appendix. A comparison of the Bell Collection copy of the former with the British Museum copy of the latter, however, shows that entire pages in the body of the text were reset. The latter edition was used as the basis for a German edition published in Cologne by Niclas Roht in 1610. From

this German edition Caspar Ens edited a Latin edition in the same year, with Cologne indicated as the place of publication by the British Museum. It includes only books 18 to 28. Also published in 1610 was the Dutch edition which contains the first account of Hudson's voyage. It bore the title *Commentarien ofte Memorien van den Nederlantsen Staet.* The second part had a separate title page. This edition is extremely rare, only the Library of Congress copy being recorded in America. It bears the fictitious imprint "Schotlandt buyten Danswyck by Hermes van Loven." Another Dutch edition with the same imprint appeared in 1611 in which the first part was titled *Nederlantsche Historien* and the second part *Belgische ofte Nederlantsche Oorlogen.* Verduyn did not know of the 1610 edition, but attributed that of 1611 to Dordrecht. See *Emanuel van Meteren,* p. 214. This 1611 Dutch edition was the basis for a German edition of Arnhem, 1612, and it is this edition in the Bell Collection which has been used in my translation. A comparison of the German text with the Dutch text of 1610 reveals only minor variations.

[21] Van Meteren's account of Hudson's voyage was first translated into English in Henry C. Murphy's *Henry Hudson in Holland* (The Hague, 1859; reprinted, The Hague, 1909). It has subsequently been translated and published several times and is included in J. Franklin Jameson, ed., *Narratives of New Netherland* (New York, 1953). My translation is not intended to be original, but owes much to Murphy's, with alterations in terms to make it conform to the language of my text.

[22] Murphy, *Henry Hudson in Holland* (1909 ed.), pp. 41–48. Plancius had kept his eye on the eastern coast of North America for some time, and had taken sufficient interest in Virginia to insert it on the second issue of his great map about 1600. He also added place names based on Thomas Hariot's *A Briefe and True Report of the New Found Land of Virginia* (London, 1588). See Frederik C. Wieder, *Monumenta Cartographica* (5 vols.; The Hague, 1925–33), plate 39. Hudson's voyage and the maps which resulted from it are discussed in I. N. Phelps Stokes, *The Iconography of Manhattan Island, 1498–1909* (6 vols.; New York, 1915–28), II, 41–61. For a reference to Van Meteren's account of the Hudson voyage see IV, 36, 37. A reproduction of the original text follows p. 48.

[23] Murphy, *Henry Hudson in Holland,* p. 47.

[24] *Ibid.,* pp. 34–44.

[25] G. M. Asher, *Henry Hudson the Navigator* (London, 1860), pp. xxvi–xxvii, states that the "real author is most probably Hudson himself" and bases his argument in part on the appearance of one second person plural usage in the narrative. The use of "we" could equally apply, it seems, to the *Half Moon* in a journal written by another person aboard.

[26] John Meredith Read, Jr., *A Historical Inquiry Concerning Henry Hudson* (Albany, 1865), pp. 150, 159.

[27] Robert Juet, *Juet's Journal,* Robert M. Lunny, ed. (Newark, 1959), p. 11.

[28] Joannes De Laet, *Nieuwe Wereldt ofte Beschrijvinghe van West-Indien* (Leiden, 1625), p. 83.

[29] *Ibid.,* p. 14.

[30] *Ibid.*, p. 22.

[31] *Ibid.*, p. 83.

[32] Juet, *Journal*, p. 29.

[33] Simon Hart, *The Prehistory of the New Netherland Company* (Amsterdam, 1959), p. 18, records that the first use of Hudson's name in connection with the river is to be found in a document of August 13, 1614, where it is referred to as "de riviere Hudson."

[34] Sir Thomas Overbury, *Observations in His Travailes* (London, 1626), p. 5.

[35] Winwood to Salisbury, 5 December 1609, in *Winwood Memorials*, III, 93–95.

[36] Edmundson, *Anglo-Dutch Rivalry*, p. 19.

[37] *Ibid.*, pp. 26–30.

[38] Van Meteren, 1612 German ed., Appendix, p. 131.

[39] This booklet of 26 pages was published by J. Stepneth. It was entered with the Company of Stationers on December 4, 1609, and published the following year.

[40] See note 20.

[41] *A True and Sincere Declaration*, p. 10.

[42] *Ibid.*

[43] *Ibid.*

[44] *Ibid.*, pp. 10–11.

[45] *Ibid.*, p. 11.

[46] Alexander Brown, *The First Republic in America* (Boston, 1898), pp. 87–88.

[47] *Ibid.*, p. 91.

[48] This is obviously a misprint, for June 18 was the date of departure according to Van Meteren's style of dating.

[49] In the 1614 edition of Van Meteren's *History* the storm is reported to have occurred one hundred fifty miles from the West Indies, and this corresponds to the English sources.

[50] This appears to be a misprint for fourteen degrees.

[51] The Dutch edition on which the German is based adds here "or these who had just arrived."

[52] Lord Delaware departed in April 1610, and in September of that year the news of the fate of the *Sea Venture* reached London. Van Meteren recorded the story of the *Sea Venture*, but not in time for this edition of his book.

[53] Van Meteren, 1612 edition, Appendix, p. 133.

STORM AND SURVIVAL

[1] Henry C. Wilkinson, *The Adventurers of Bermuda* (London, 1958), p. 21.

[2] Don Alonso de Velasco to Philip III of Spain, 14 June 1610, in Brown, *Genesis*, I, 392.

[3] William Crashaw, *A Sermon Preached in London before the . . . Lord Lawarr* (London, 1610).

[4] *Ibid.*, fol. C2 recto.

[5] *Ibid.*, fol. D2 recto.

[6] *Ibid.*, fol. C3 recto.

[7] *Ibid.*, fol. D4 recto.

[8] *Ibid.*, fol. E2 verso.

[9] *Ibid.*, fol. E4 verso.

[10] *Ibid.*, fol. G1 recto.

[11] *Ibid.*, fol. G2 recto.

[12] *Ibid.*, fol. H4 verso.

[13] For comments on the relationship of *The Tempest* to the Bermuda episode and the colonization of Virginia see Richard Garnett, "The Date and Occasion of *The Tempest*" in his *Essays of an Ex-Librarian* (London, 1901), pp. 31–54.

[14] Richard Rich, *Newes from Virginia. The Lost Flocke Triumphant* (London, 1610), fol. A4 recto.

[15] Silvester Jourdain, *A Discovery of the Barmudas* (London, 1610).

[16] *A True Declaration of the Estate of the Colonie in Virginia* (London, 1610).

[17] The *Sea Venture* apparently was a ship of about 290 tons, with a length of 108 feet. It was built for the Virginia Company at a cost of some 1200 pounds, Sir George Somers being the major holder with 300 pounds invested in the construction of the ship. See Wilkinson, *Adventurers of Bermuda*, p. 43.

[18] *A True Declaration*, p. 21.

[19] Jourdain, *Discovery of the Barmudas*, p. 5.

[20] William Strachey's narrative is quoted in Wilkinson, *Adventurers of Bermuda*, p. 46.

[21] The presence of hogs on Bermuda has been attributed to ships wrecked while taking the animals to settlements in Spanish colonies. These animals were well remembered, for when in 1615 the Somers Island Company was formed for the settling of Bermuda they struck off some coins bearing a hog on one side and a ship on the other.

[22] The girl, Bermuda, was the daughter of John Rolfe, who was later to become the husband of Pocahontas. There appear to have been only five deaths among the group during the time they were on the island.

[23] Salisbury to Winwood, 3 December 1609, in Historical Manuscripts Commission, *Report on the Manuscripts of the Duke of Buccleuch and Queensberry*, I, 83.

[24] *Ibid.*

[25] *Ibid.*, I, 97.

[26] See below, p. 77.

[27] Jourdain and the *True Declaration* both give the number of survivors as 150.

[28] Eleven men shared the ownership of the Bermuda colony at its beginning, but they were soon joined by seven others. Among this membership were six investors in the East India Company. Sir Thomas Smith, treasurer of the Virginia Company, was made governor.

[29] For the first few years, the major interest of the Bermuda group was ambergris, a solid fatty substance of variegated gray and black color, secreted from the

abdomen of the spermaceti whale. It is found floating on the ocean or cast up on shore, and is used primarily in perfumes.

[30] Wilkinson, *Adventurers of Bermuda*, p. 60.

[31] Peter Martyr d'Anghiera, *Opera* [Seville, 1511], unsigned leaf after fol. f8.

[32] This was the Huguenot colony established by Jean Ribaut in 1562. It was during his absence in England where he tried to gain English support for this anti-Spanish undertaking that Mendenez fell upon the colony and wiped it out.

[33] Lord Delaware and the Council of Virginia to the Virginia Company of London, 7 July 1610, in Brown, *Genesis*, I, 407.

[34] *Ibid.*, p. 411.

[85] Thomas West, Baron Delaware, *The Relation of the Right Honorable the Lord De-La-Warre, Lord Governor and Captain General of the Colonie, Planted in Virginia* (London, 1611), fol. A4, recto, verso.

[36] Alonso de Velasco to Philip III of Spain, 30 September 1610, in Brown, *Genesis*, I, 418–419.

[37] This exacting code of laws was edited by William Strachey, entered with the Stationers Company on August 13, 1611, and published the following year.

[38] O'Callaghan, *Documents Relative to the Colonial History of . . . New York*, I, 2.

[39] It is generally believed that the name "Dutch Gap" pertains to German artisans who were brought to Virginia in 1608, and who had a glass factory of sorts there. The term "Dutch" was commonly applied to Germans at that time. Brock, "Virginia, 1606–1689," p. 138.

[40] *Ibid.*, p. 138.

[41] Quoted in Brown, *Genesis*, II, 870.

[42] Walter F. Prince, "The First Criminal Code of Virginia," *Annual Report of the American Historical Association* (Washington, D.C., 1900), pp. 309–363, discussed the origins of the code and attributed the major responsibility for its formulation to Gates and Dale, denying, however, that it was based entirely on a Dutch military code as is sometimes alleged.

[43] More to Winwood, 12 December 1610, in *Winwood Memorials*, III, 239–240.

[44] Arthur P. Newton, *The Colonising Activities of the English Puritans* (New Haven, 1914), p. 26. English activities in Guiana were also watched with interest by Emanuel van Meteren, and his *History* included information on that segment of England's interest in the New World which was not published in any English book of the period.

[45] More to Winwood, 12 December 1610, in *Winwood Memorials*, III, 239–240.

[46] Francis Cottington to William Trumbull, 10 January 1611, in *Winwood Memorials*, III, 250. Trumbull was the English ambassador at Brussels.

[47] *State Papers, Spain*, 94/18:220.

[48] More to Winwood, 29 November 1611, in *Winwood Memorials*, III, 309.

[49] Winwood to Salisbury, 10 March 1612, *State Papers, Holland*, 84/68:252–253.

[50] De Laet, *Nieuwe Wereldt*, p. 84. Simon Hart in his book *The Prehistory of the New Netherland Company*, p. 18, discounts entirely De Laet's report of this voyage. Hart points to the fact that De Laet began with the words "After Hendrick Hudson returned to Amsterdam with his report in the year 1610 . . ." This is obviously an error on the part of De Laet, since Hudson was not permitted to return. The information, however, surely got to Amsterdam; Dutch members of the crew were not restrained, and Emanuel van Meteren had the account of the voyage in print the following year, so he could have sent it to the directors of the Dutch East India Company in Amsterdam.

[51] Quoted in Hart, *The Prehistory of the New Netherland Company*, p. 18. The term "River Montagnes," with several variations in spelling, was used on early maps showing the Hudson River. "Mauritius" is used on a map of 1614. The earliest use of Hudson's name with the river is in a document of August 13, 1614. See Hart, p. 18.

[52] S. Muller, ed., *De Reis van Jan Cornelisz May* (The Hague, 1909).

[53] Hart, *The Prehistory of the New Netherland Company*, pp. 22–24.

[54] See also Phelps Stokes, *Iconography of Manhattan Island*, III, pp. 63–75.

[55] Van Meteren, 1614 edition, fol. 670 verso.

[56] Dale to Salisbury, 17 August 1611, in Brown, *Genesis*, I, 501–508.

[57] Velasco to Philip III, 22 August 1611, in Brown, *Genesis*, I, 494–495. In a letter of 17 June 1611 (Brown, *Genesis*, I, 476), Philip had ordered his ambassador to secure "two Catholic men, in whom you can perfectly trust," to send to Virginia.

[58] Philip III to Velasco, 25 February 1612, in Brown, *Genesis*, II, 537–538.

[59] Sir John Digby to Salisbury, 2 February 1612, in Brown, *Genesis*, II, 536. Digby was ambassador to Spain from April 1611 to January 1616. He was a subscriber to the Virginia Company, was a member of the Northwest Passage Company of 1612, and in general took a keen interest in English overseas activities.

[60] Digby to Salisbury, 9 March 1612, in Brown, *Genesis*, II, 539.

[61] G. N. Clark and Jonkheer W. J. M. Van Eysinga, *The Colonial Conferences between England and the Netherlands in 1613 and 1615* (Leiden, 1940), pp. 41–44. This work is volume 32 in the *Bibliotheca Visseriana* series.

[62] Salisbury to Winwood, 4 January 1612, in *State Papers, Holland*, 84/68:213.

[63] Winwood to Salisbury, 31 January 1612, in *State Papers, Holland*, 84/68: 229–230. This is published in Clark and Van Eysinga, pp. 51–52, but with slight differences, and I believe the quotation here corresponds more closely to the original document. Winwood's version of the right of commerce was that commerce "tira sa source du droict des gens laquelle n'est borneé ny des limites du jure ny du temps, ains passe librement par tout l'univers, et est communicable a lout la monde."

[64] No less a Spain-hater than Sir Thomas Dale found himself fighting against the Dutch in the East Indies when he sailed there with a fleet in 1618 and encountered Dutch ships in "a cruel bloody fight" near Java on December 25 of that year (Brown, *Genesis*, II, 873).

INDEX

Soto, Hernando de, 42

Spain: administration of Netherlands, 7; relations with England, 11, 20–21, 24, 34, 38, 78; reaction to Virginia settlement, 25, 33–34, 36–37, 81; alliance with France, 38; reinforces troops in southern Netherlands, 81. *See also* Netherlands war of liberation; Velasco, Don Alonso; Zuñiga, Pedro de

Spencer, Sir Richard, 23, 34, 37

States-General: and Van Meteren's *History*, 17; controlled by cities, 22, 26; and Dutch West India Company, 35; weakness of, 62; and peace in East Indies, 82; mentioned, 10, 40

Stuyvesant, Peter, 3

Symonds, William, 41

Tempest, The, 65

Tremillius, Emanuel, 8

Trinidad, 62

True and Sincere Declaration . . . 53–55, 58

True Declaration of . . . Virginia, A, 65

Tyndale, William, 7

Usselinx, Willem: proposal for Dutch West India Company, 15, 16, 22, 30, 34; opposed to peace with Spain, 38; mentioned, 25, 32

Velasco, Don Alonso de: recommends destruction of Virginia settlement, 61, 75, 77–78; plans to place spies on English ships, 81

Vennecool, Cornelisz, 17

Virginia: Anglo-Dutch collaboration in, 4; exploration of, 25, 29–30; first

charter, 25, 26–29, 30; reaction of Spain to settlement in, 25, 33–34, 36–37, 81; northern colony, 27, 59; description, 29–30, 68; settlement in *1607*, 29–30, 32–33; Dutch interest in, 32, 78–79; second charter, 40; voyages of *1609*, 52–60; weakness of government, 68, 73–74; settlement abandoned by Gates, 69; sickness among colonists, 74. *See also* Velasco, Don Alonso; Zuñiga, Pedro de

Virginia, Council of, established, 25

Wassenaer, Nicolaes à, 79

West, Thomas, *see* Delaware, Lord

Weymouth, Capt. George, 15, 25, 47

William of Orange, 12

Wingfield, Edward Maria, 26, 29, 31, 36

Winwood, Sir Ralph: at truce conference, 23, 34, 37; reports Dutch colonization in East Indies, 50; asked to assist Gates, 70, 71; letter from John More, 77, 78; seeks collaboration with Dutch in East Indies, 78; presents case of East Indian merchants, 82

Wood, Benjamin, 87 n35

Wool trade, Anglo-Dutch, 4, 5, 6

Worde, Wynkyn de, 7

Wytfliet, Corneille, 14

Ybarra, Pedro de, 55

Zuñiga, Pedro de: reports plans for Virginia settlement, 25; fears Dutch in Virginia, 33; sees Virginia as pirate base, 34; reports plans for Virginia settlement in *1609*, 42

THIS *book, in Linotype Times Roman on Mohawk Superfine Text, was designed by Jane McCarthy of the University of Minnesota Press. It was composed and printed at the Lund Press, Minneapolis and bound at the National Bookbinding Company Stevens Point, Wisconsin. Of the limited edition of 750 copies this is copy* 482